This book is lovingly dedicated to

the memory of my mother

Brenda Griffiths

and

to my grandchildren

Calan Griffiths and Ava Gambino

'The survival of the Welsh nation is something of a miracle. From the fourth to the fifteenth century the theme running through the history of Wales is the struggle, often heroic, to defend and maintain its identity.'

Gwynfor Evans, President of Plaid Cymru (1945–81), Hon. President (1982–2005), Member of Parliament for Carmarthen (1966–70 and 1974–9).

'There is a tendency to forget the great men of a conquered race. They are judged by the failure of their aims, once independence, that boon of peoples, is lost. They toiled indeed in the heat of the day; they seemed to live but for their country's weal; they fought and died in its defence; but of what avail was it all, when the day of doom came, and that which they had laboured to preserve was lost for ever?'

Professor Paul Barbier, *The Age of Owain Gwynedd.*

FOREWORD

The history of Wales between the years 1063 and 1283 is dominated by incessant warfare between the native rulers of Wales and powerful invaders from England. During this era, a period of history since defined as 'The Age of the Welsh Princes', these brave native leaders, with limited resources, were openly confronted by the powerful might of alien expansionists. In essence, from the time of the arrival of the Roman armies on Welsh soil, near the end of the first century AD, until the climax of Owain Glyndŵr's failed 'rebellion' in 1415, a period spanning more than 1,300 years, almost every European tribe, clan or race imaginable had occupied or raided the land now known as Wales. The battleground that Wales became also witnessed sporadic warfare between the native rulers of the various Welsh kingdoms, whose appetite for gain and conquest appeared to be no different to that of the invaders. During such turbulent times, the gentle surface of the countryside was trodden over roughshod by the movement of hundreds, and sometimes thousands, of marching feet: Roman legions from overseas, fearsome Picts from the north, savage Viking raiders and marauders from nearby Ireland, each leaving behind a bloodied imprint on the landscape of Wales.

As the centuries passed, there dawned the era of the Anglo Saxons, a war-mongering combination of peoples from northern Europe who craved power and supremacy beyond their natural borders, followed by Norman invaders from northern France, whose mail-clad ranks routinely dined on terror and territory. During these seemingly endless waves of violent raids and campaigns, the course of everyday life for the inhabitants of Wales must have been unbearable. In reality, the short-term havoc created by a raid or battle did not end there. Religious buildings were looted of their sacred contents, vital provisions were stolen and ordinary dwellings ransacked. Fields brimming with crops planted by local inhabitants were put to the torch and herds of livestock driven away. Even worse, scores of innocent people were carried into captivity to be used as slaves.

In northern Wales, the numerous campaigns, conflicts and conquests created a proliferation of native hill forts, Mercian dykes, Norman motte and bailey castles and stone fortifications throughout the landscape. As a result of the construction of these military buildings, Wales is said to have more castles per square mile than any other country in the world. In the region of north-east Wales, battles were reputedly fought at Chester(616), Morfa Rhuddlan (796), Coleshill (1150) and Denbigh (1294), and the battle with the highest profile fought in that area was undoubtedly the clash of arms that took place at Coleshill in 1157, between the forces of King Henry II of England and Prince Owain Gwynedd of Wales. Based upon the available evidence, Henry's military expedition into the interior of north-east Wales proved an ill-fated affair. Intended to reverse the growing power of Prince Owain, the ruler of Gwynedd, the campaign was a typically savage affair, sprinkled with high drama and tactical daring. The King's plans were well laid and remarkably advanced for the period; a strong naval force would support the large land army as it progressed along the coastline of north-east Wales and, during the summer of 1157, he entered Wales via Chester at the head of a considerable force. He came under attack alomost immediately by a body of what can best be described as Welsh 'guerilla fighters.' The daring attack that took place somewhere within the woodlands of Tegeingl (in what was later to become Flintshire) proved that the outcome of carefully planned manoeuvres, orchestrated by a much smaller force, could in fact prove successful. The engagement at 'Coleshill' proved to be the pivotal moment of the campaign. In essence, when Owain Gwynedd ordered his men to attack the king's troops so close to the border with England, the immediate future of Welsh resistance lay in the balance. Had the Welsh troops been defeated, it is more than probable that Welsh resistance would have crumbled.

A notable battle in which a Welsh ruler intentionally confronted a king of England in such a manner is to be regarded as an historic rarity. This remarkable campaign, between two highly motivated, strong-minded and capable commanders, stretched along the entire coastline of northern Wales, from the marshes of Chester to the beaches of Anglesey.

More than 860 years have passed since the Battle of Coleshill was fought and this account has been constructed using material sourced from mediaeval chronicles, contemporary poetry, oral traditions and works penned by the hand of highly regarded historians. Any errors of fact or interpretation in the text are entirely my own.

Steve Griffiths
Hawarden, 2018

1

When invading troops led by the Emperor Claudius of Rome (d 54AD) set foot upon the shores of Britain in the year 43AD, the ensuing military occupation of the majority of the island would last for the next three-and-a-half centuries. By the end of the fourth century AD, Rome was deeply embroiled in the defence of her territories, a crisis that caused the garrison of Britain to be gradually withdrawn to help with the flagging fortunes of the dwindling empire. In the wake of the Roman withdrawal, the indigenous inhabitants of Britain appeared to be at the dawn of a new era: the Christian religion flourished, established towns valued order and security, simple industries thrived and a network of roads aided travel and trade. As further confirmation of Roman influence, a golden age of learning and literature appeared to have taken root.

The opportunity for stability and growth was, however, thwarted by a series of foreign incursions. Shortly after the final withdrawal of Roman power in 410AD, the inhabitants of the less Romanised regions of Britain — the areas that would later become Wales and the northern marches — gained local military leaders who ambitiously sought power for their own dynasties. According to tradition, a fifth-century British ruler called Vortigern (the Gwrtheyrn of Welsh tradition) summoned the aid of Germanic mercenary soldiers in his war against the uncontrollable Picts of northern Britain. In essence, the possibility of yet another conquest had not been foreseen by the native Britons, but the hired mercenaries who came, readily turned themselves into a community of permanent colonists, thereby establishing a

The remains of the Roman amphitheatre in Chester.

Germanic toe-hold in Britain. Writing a century later, Gildas, a monk and author of *De Excidio Britanniae* [On the Ruin and Conquest of Britain], boiled with indignation:

> To hold back the northern peoples, they introduced into the island the vile unspeakable Saxons, hated of God and man alike ... What raw hopeless stupidity! Of their own free will, they invited under the same roof the enemy they feared worse than death.

During the earliest mediaeval period, 400–800 AD, sporadic warfare erupted between the various tribes, native royal houses and lesser kingdoms of Britain. It is not unreasonable to name this particular period of Britain's history as 'The Age of the Germanico-Celtic Isles', a period which witnessed the irreconcilable division of the island into three portions: a Brythonic west, a Teutonic east, and a Gaelic north. Of the mixed bag of Germanic tribes who arrived in Britain, it was the Saxons, the Angles, and the Jutes who provided the island with the greater part of its migrants. In time, a series of Germanic kingdoms crystallised creating the still recognisable entities of Kent, Essex, Sussex, Wessex and Mercia. In this matrix of cultural change, the native tribes continued on their traditional course of disunity, which aided the growth of Germanic expansionism. The Picts from the far north descended southwards to conduct a chain of violent raids on native Britons and Germanics alike, and Celtic pirates from Ireland, called Scotti, randomly attacked the western coasts.

The Germanic advances were particularly successful in the south-eastern corner of Britain where the Celtic speech of the natives was drowned in the rising tide of Germanic dialects, never to resurface again. However, one of the most popular oversimplifications of this period is to reduce the complex interplay of peoples to a straightforward confrontation between Celts and Germanics. In the shifting kaleidoscope of alliances, in-fighting appears to have been widespread between factions on both sides, as the Angles sometimes battled with the Saxons, Saxons often battled other Saxon groups, and the ruling Celtic warlords willingly fought against their neighbouring Celtic warlords on numerous occasions.

Sometime during or around the year 616, a crucial battle took place at Chester between an army of native Britons and a large force led by Aethelfrith, the first king of the Germanic kingdom of Northumbria [North of the Humber]. On the eve of the battle, the pagan Aethelfrith issued his troops a license to slaughter unarmed monks which resulted in the massacre of 1200 monks who had been praying for their fellow Britons prior to the battle. The slaughter of so many paved the way for a resounding victory for the Northumbrians. This major defeat resulted in the geographical separation of the Britons in the north — now Scotland and Cumbria— from those who resided in the western part of Britain — now Wales and the West Country.

The original Germanic settlements then commanded the great lowland areas that were rich in agriculture and the major trading centres. The settlers' ravenous appetite for additional land knew no bounds and the kingdom of Mercia emerged as the dominant of the Germanic kingdoms south of the Humber. During the eighth and ninth centuries the Mercian kings began to colonise westwards from Chester, penetrating the valleys of the Dee, the Wye and the Severn. This territorial development created a new friction as the newly formed Mercian settlements were openly vulnerable to dangerous attacks from the western Britons. The escalating turbulence between these two peoples resulted in the construction by the Mercians of a massive earthen bank and ditch (Wat's Dyke) sometime between the years 650 and 750. The defensive dyke extended for 40 miles from the Severn Valley northwards towards the estuary of the Dee. The Mercians followed this enormous enterprise by the building of an even greater dyke (Offa's Dyke) during the reign of Offa, King of Mercia (ruled 757–96) which extended for 130 miles from near Bristol in the south to near Flint in the north (sections of both earthworks are still visible today). The elaborate creation of a large-scale,

A surviving section of Wat's Dyke in New Brighton, near Mold.

fixed frontier between the two cultures, however, could not fail to have far-reaching consequences. In all probability, it was initially constructed to give respite from the Britons. Instead, it realistically ensured that the 'western men' would never escape from the isolation of their mountainous peninsula; that their precious language and culture would develop in directions not shared by the other Celtic groups; and the future would hand them a separate national identity. But, who were these 'western men'?

2

Tradition maintains that sometime during the mid-fifth century, a Celtic tribe from north of Hadrian's Wall, the Votadini, seized the island of Anglesey where the tribe's chieftain and commander, Cunedda, laid the foundations of what was to become the royal dynasty of Gwynedd (the Votadini were known in the Welsh language as the Gododdin). In line with this tradition, a number of Cunedda's sons and grandsons gave their names to various regions of northern Wales, including Meirionydd (Meirion), Rhufoniog (Rhufen), Ceredigion (Ceredig) and Edeirnion (Edern). This legend rests on rather shaky foundations and lacks conclusive proof. In spite of this, there were a number of native political authorities in existence in the territories that later became Wales around the time of the Roman withdrawal, which formed a number of relatively small independent kingdoms in their own right. In other areas of Britain, the Germanic tribes had already achieved a number of territorial gains. In Wales, however, these early native kingdoms survived the Germanic threat. These early kingdoms included Gwynedd in north-west Wales, Powys in central Wales, Dyfed in south-west Wales and Gwent in south-east Wales. United by their Christian faith, culture, customs and treasured language (in 400 AD, they spoke the primitive British tongue; by the year 700 AD, they spoke the unmistakeable language which we know today as Welsh), these isolated western Britons possessed an implacable determination to defend their territory, their way of life and their freedoms at all costs. The native name for their country, *Cymru*, means 'land of the *Cymry*' which itself originates from the Brythonic word *Combrogi* meaning

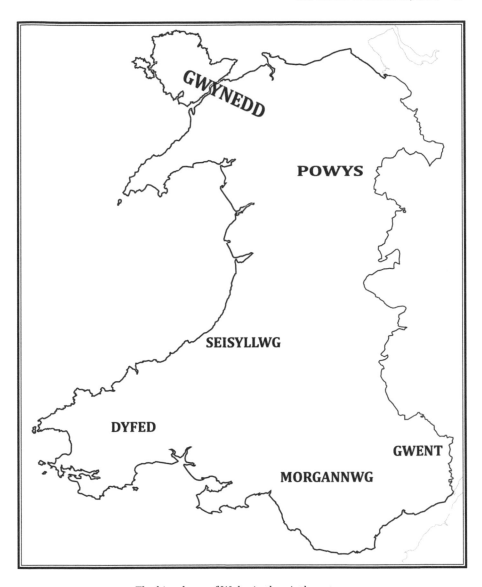

The kingdoms of Wales in the ninth century.
During the phased arrival in Britain of several powerful Germanic tribes, including
the Saxons, Angles and Jutes, the mainland witnessed the irreconcilable division
of its peoples into three regions: the Brthyonic west (later Wales), the Teutonic east
(later England) and the Gaelic north (later Scotland).

'men of the same country', and between 500 and 700 AD, Brythonic Britain effectively came to an end and early *Cymru* began to emerge. Likewise, the word *Cymry*, meaning 'the Welsh people', gradually came to represent the peoples of Wales, ousting the previous word *Brythoniaid*. In contrast, further east, an alternative word was being used to describe the Britons or *Cymry* in the West. The newly-settled, Germanic-speaking tribes referred to these native peoples as *Waelisc*, a word meaning 'foreigner, stranger, those different to us', while their land was known as *Wealas*. These two words developed into the English words 'Welsh' and 'Wales'. Collectively, the Germanic tribes are better known to history as the Anglo-Saxons or Saxons (this being the dominant tribe) and from this combination of tribes we get an evolution from the words *Engle* to Angles or *Englisc* to Anglisc. In essence, by the year 800, the conditions had been created whereby Wales, England, Scotland and Ireland could all begin to develop as separate nations.

Wales was a land of many kingdoms and dynasties, and no single Welsh ruler had ever been dominant enough to take control of the entire country. Of the pantheon of Welsh rulers who lived, reigned, and fought during the period 800–1063, only three of their number succeeded in forging a realm which covered an extensive surface area of Wales: Rhodri Fawr (Rhodri the Great, d 878), king of Gwynedd and ruler of Powys and Ceredigion; Hywel Dda (Hywel the Good, d 949/950), ruler of the kingdoms of Seisyllwg (consisting of Ceredigion and Ystrad Tywi), Dyfed (roughly synonymous with modern Pembrokeshire), Gwynedd, and possibly, Powys; and Gruffudd ap Llywelyn (d 1063), king of Gwynedd and Deheubarth, and ruler of Powys, Morgannwg (Glamorgan) and possibly Gwent. From the period of the Roman withdrawal from Britain in 410, to the arrival of William the Conqueror's invading army in 1066, these three Welsh kings of extraordinary quality, who ruled almost a century apart from one another, are regarded as Wales' most dominant figures.

On 5 August 1063, Wales was dealt a devastating body blow when King

Gruffudd ap Llywelyn met a violent death at the hands of a fellow Welshman. Following Gruffudd's death, his head was hacked from his broken body and the macabre trophy transported in triumph to his royal enemies in England. The head was initially taken to Earl Harold of Wessex, and then delivered to Edward the Confessor. Tragically, it was weakness from within, rather than strength from outside, which had brought about Gruffudd's inglorious end. During the course of his spectacular career, he had succeeded in unifying the disjointed kingdoms and mini-kingdoms of Wales into the reality of a self-governing nation, and his supremacy enabled him to embark on an aggressive campaign against the Crown of England. While blazing a path to total dominance, Gruffudd created his own legend by the process of military endeavour, political astuteness and sheer ruthlessness. In 1055, in alliance with the Mercians, Gruffudd captured Hereford Castle in a surprise attack. The city, including its cathedral, was put to the torch. On 16 June 1056, he won another victory near Glasbury-on-Wye in the valley of the Machawy (Bachawy) against an army led by Leofgar, the bishop of Hereford. Following the death of King Gruffudd ap Llywelyn, the out-pouring of tributes proved plentiful. The twelfth-century writer Walter Map, a cleric from Herefordshire, compared Gruffudd with Alexander the Great; whilst the Welsh chronicle *Brut y Tywysogyon* saluted this seemingly 'invincible' king as 'the head and shield and defender of the Britons.' An English chronicle recorded – 'They [the Welsh] are too strong while Gruffudd is king over them.' The eminent Welsh historian J. E. Lloyd, praised him – 'He founded no dynasty, but he bequeathed to the Welsh people the priceless legacy of a revived national spirit.'

Gruffudd's bloody death returned Wales to its traditional pattern of multiple kingships and fierce domestic rivalries, and within a few years the land of Wales had plummeted into the dark abyss of civil war. As the bitter conflict between a throng of dynastic claimants and opportunist usurpers raged, the fabric of Gruffudd's former impressive realm was torn to pieces.

On the eve of the infamous cycle of bloody hostilities that can only be regarded as a Welsh civil war, an assembly of Welsh rulers and senior nobles stood poised to hurle headlong into a murderous fight for power. In essence, the kingdom of Gruffudd ap Llywelyn had fragmented into five independent mini-kingdoms. The kingdoms of Gwynedd and Powys were joined together as a single entity beneath the shared rulership of the half-brothers of Gruffudd ap Llywelyn, Rhiwallon (d 1069) and Bleddyn ap Cynfyn (d 1075). In central Wales, the small kingdom of Arwystli was held by the highly ambitious Trahaearn ap Caradog (d 1081), and the southern portion of Wales played host to three prominent kingdoms: Deuheubarth in the south-west, controlled by Maredudd ab Owain (d 1072); Gwent and Gwynllwg in the south-east, held by the much feared Caradog ap Gruffudd (d 1081); and Morgannwg, the upland territory between the Taff and the Neath, controlled by Cadwgan ap Meurig. Akin to a seething nest of vipers, these men discharged their deathly venom upon all who purposely crossed the marked boundaries of their respective realms.

The year 1069 signalled the genesis of the Welsh civil war and, until its conclusion some twelve years later, the pages of Welsh history were daubed crimson by an outpouring of blood. At Mechain, in Powys, the scene of the opening slaughter, the spirited bravery displayed on the battlefield by Gruffudd ap Llywelyn's two young warrior sons ultimately failed to curb the rising power of Bleddyn ap Cynfyn; Ithel ap Llywelyn perished on the field of battle, whilst his severely wounded brother, Maredudd, died later from exposure after fleeing the slaughter. For the victorious Bleddyn ap Cynfyn, who now emerged as the solitary ruler of Gwynedd and Powys, this hard won triumph was somewhat tainted by the death on the battlefield of his brother, Rhiwallon.

The bloodshed continued as the hills and valleys of Wales played host to a series of follow-up battles, including equally destructive engagements at Rhymney (1072), Camddwr (1075), Bron-yr-Erw (1075), Gweunytwl (1077) and Pwll-Gwdig (1078). Among the many that fell during these and other murderous encounters on the killing fields of Wales, were such notables as Maredudd ab Owain, Bleddyn ap Cynfyn, Rhydderch ap Caradog, Rhys ap Owain and Hywel ab Owain.

By the year 1081, this civil war, which was in its twelfth year, had reached its climax and only four principal royal claimants remained. A confederated army led by Trahaearn ap Caradog of Arwystli, the ruling king of Gwynedd, and Caradog ap Gruffudd, the king of Gwent and Morgannwg, took to the field of battle determined to quash the ambition of two principal enemies, namely Gruffudd ap Cynan, a claimant to the throne of Gwynedd, and Rhys ap Tewdwr of Deheubarth. The defining clash of arms took place at Mynydd Carn, a place probably in the Preseli Mountains of north Pembrokeshire. At the end of the battle, Trahaearn and Caradog lay dead and their forces had been destroyed. This hotly contested encounter ensured that the two victors and their respective descendants would permanently control their dynastic territories. The battle had an important and lasting effect on Welsh history as Gruffudd's rise to power and prominence signalled the resurrection of the northern Welsh kingdom of Gwynedd, an achievement which produced a royal dynasty whose bloodline would maintain itself and flourish for the next two hundred years. Sadly, the fledgling kingships of Grufffudd ap Cynan of Gwynedd and Rhys ap Tewdwr of Deheubarth did not enjoy harmonious beginnings, as a new and far greater threat to Wales had newly materialised in the form of a war-mongering race of people from northern France, more commonly known as the Normans.

3

On a clear autumn day in 1066, more than 7,000 iron-clad men of war were packed tightly together aboard a vast fleet of more than seven hundred ships in the French port of St Valery at the mouth of the river Somme. Finally blessed with favourable conditions, the fleet weighed anchors on 27 September and sailed towards England. Carrying a huge consignment of provisions, including weaponry, armour, food and horses, the floating Norman war machine was ably led by its brilliantly gifted commander William, duke of Normandy (Guillame le Batard, or in English William the Bastard). Driven by a favourable wind, this giant armada of Viking-style 'longships' reached the bay of Pevensey in eastern Sussex. After dropping anchor, the assembled occupants frantically dashed ashore like a herd of wild animals, visibly transforming the gentle blue waters of the English bay into a bubbling cauldron of snow white foam. In the absence of any English armed resistance, the thousands of enemy soldiers stepped on to the English shore unopposed. Duke William's meticulous planning for such a gargantuan invasion was faultless; sergeants and sailors yelled instructions to squires and soldiers, as war-horses and palfreys (among 2,000 travelling horses) were forced over the sides of the 25-metre long vessels and guided ashore. Elsewhere, the skilled carpenters landed with great axes in their hands, so too the corps of archers, each with his bow strung and a quiver full of arrows dangling menacingly from his side. Finally, the knights landed, kitted in their expensively crafted chain-mail and coloured tabards, their wooden, kite-shaped shields were slung at their necks and their polished conical helmets laced. As the thousands of Norman soldiers busily scoured the idyllic English countryside for a glimpse of the English royal army, Harold, the king of Anglo-Saxon England, was in fact many miles away, near York and was suffering greatly from battle fatigue from an earlier engagement on 25 September, against a large army of Vikings at Stamford Bridge, near York. Upon hearing the shocking news of the Norman invasion of southern England, Harold ordered his exhausted and badly mauled army to rise again to face the challenge of another significant battle. The admirable march southwards along the Old Roman road by King Harold's royal army from Stamford Bridge to Hastings is one of the grandest epics of English history. Marching at an incredible pace, by both day and night, they covered the 250 miles in only twelve days.

On the morning of 14 October, St Callixtus's Day, the two armies collided in battle at a place called Senlac Hill (sometimes known as Senlac Ridge) in Sussex, some seven miles north-west of the town of Hastings. This battle was to shape the future of mediaeval England. The exact numbers present at the battle are unknown, but the composition of the forces is clear. Harold's army was composed almost entirely of infantry and possessed few archers, whereas only half of the invading force was infantry, the remainder being split equally between mounted cavalry and archers.

As the battle began, the Normans' superbly drilled, mail-clad horsemen smashed into the defensive formation of Harold's mile-long shield wall, a manoeuvre which the horsemen repeated time and again. The Normans were stunned by the gallantry of the English resistance, and had never before encountered an enemy who possessed such courage and resolute conviction. Hour upon hour of savage combat followed as the pendulum of success swung precariously from one side to the other. After almost eight hours into the exhaustive fight, and with dusk fast approaching, the balance suddenly swung in William's favour. The duke instructed his archers to aim their arrows high into the sky in order to overcome Harold's thus far impenetrable shield wall. As volley after murderous volley began to decimate Harold's ranks, William cunningly executed an additional tactic. Upon his command, his cavalry suddenly feigned retreat. This cleverly enacted sham hoodwinked the ranks of the English infantry, who broke formation to spontaneously chase the fleeing Normans. As they did so, the Norman bowmen continued to release arrows into Harold's exposed ranks. Reforming, the Norman horsemen then began to dominate the disorganised English army, paving the way for a sensational victory on foreign soil. In the face of such overwhelming pressure, English resistance eventually buckled and the day was William's. Two of the king's brothers, Gyrthe and Leofwyne, were amongst the estimated 10,000 slain on the battlefield.

As the victors scoured the battlefield for souvenirs and grim trophies, they stumbled upon the mangled body of King Harold among the blood and broken shields. The final fate of the body remains shrouded in mystery, but one account records that shortly after the battle a small English delegation, fronted by Harold's former wife, Edith Swan-Neck (Edith the Fair), claimed the near-naked body of their fallen king and, delicately wrapping him into a purple burial shroud, solemnly carried him from the historic field of battle. Whatever the truth of the matter, as the royal corpse disappeared from sight, all Anglo-Saxon hopes of ruling the kingdom of England collapsed.

Following the epic battle at Hastings, the victorious Duke William, now known in his native French tongue as *Le Conquerant*, the conqueror, steadfastly imposed his will and rule on his conquered lands and began the Normanisation of Anglo-Saxon England. To consolidate his hold over his newly acquired kingdom, wealthy English landowners were systematically stripped of their estates and their properties transferred on a golden plate of conquest to a select group of William's trusted Norman lieutenants, instigating a colossal programme of expropriation. His policy of subjugating Anglo-Saxon England via the trusted medium of theft, terror and murder, rewarded William handsomely. On Christmas Day, 1066, he was crowned

King William I of England during a lavish ceremony conducted within the grandeur of London's Westminster Abbey. The coronation of a Norman as king of England signalled the birth of the feudal state of *Angleterre*, and during the years that followed, the Norman hierarchy deliberately overwhelmed England's traditional machinery of state with an avalanche of Norman customs and laws, and the entire ruling class submitted to the new system. Even the Church accepted the French tongue as the first language of the state. It is a recognised fact that the Norman knights who had accompanied William to the Hastings battlefield were equally as ambitious as their triumphant leader and, having been granted permission by the new king to grab all the land they could manage, these Norman nobles proceeded to occupy great swathes of the English countryside. Within a short space of time, the brute strength of the Norman lord was recognisably superior to that of the English nobleman. Tens of thousands of manors, large and small, passed into French hands, and all but two of the new king's senior tenants hailed from France. The English submission that had begun at Hastings, gathered momentum after William's coronation, as every rebellious Anglo-Saxon outpost still offering resistance was brutally quashed. The city of Chester, considered to be one of the final stations to oppose the new king, eventually submitted during the winter of 1070 after a Norman attack on the city resulted in the hostile burning of over two hundred of the city's dwellings. As the victorious King William climbed the stone steps leading to Chester's historic walls, he would not have failed to observe the nearby hills and mountains of northern Wales. From that moment onwards, the Normans trained their sights westwards towards the mist-shrouded peaks of neighbouring Wales.

4

King William and his entourage had successfully conquered England in the short period of four dynamic years. He then needed to protect the entire length of his kingdom's vulnerable border with the Welsh kingdoms to the west. In order to control this important frontier, or in French – *marche* – William created three important earldoms. The strategic towns of Chester, Shrewsbury and Hereford, would form an ideal platform for military forays into Wales and William duly gave control of this area to a fearsome collection of some of the most beligerent Norman nobles of the period, some of whom were veterans of the Hastings blood-bath. Hugh d'Avranches (d 1101), otherwise known as Hugh Lupus (Hugh the Wolf) or *le Gros*, (the Fat), became earl of Chester in around 1070. He worked in close partnership with his cousin, Robert de Tillieul (d 1093, better known as Robert of Rhuddlan), and between them they controlled the city of Chester and the large county of Cheshire. Roger de Montgomery (d 1094), a personal friend to William, became the earl of Shrewsbury. William Fitzosbern (d 1071), a relative of William and a veteran of Hastings, took control of the earldom of Hereford. Supported by an army of retainers, Fitzosbern began an ambitious castle-building policy, erecting fortresses at Monmouth, Wigmore, Clifford and Ewyas Harold. King William built his lasting empire on a personal philosophy of 'Destroy your enemies and waste their country; let everything be set alight by flame and burning, leave nothing for them ... on which they could have dinner...this is how war should be begun.' These loyal adherents of such a brutal ruler would focus their efforts on the land of Wales, a country that had

*Statue of William the Conqueror
at Falaise in Normandy.*

only recently undergone the damaging episode of a savagely fought civil war.

After Gruffudd ap Cynan's impressive victory at the battle of Mynydd Carn in 1081, the newly crowned ruler of the northern kingdom of Gwynedd could not afford to bask in the sunshine of his triumph as the Normans were determined to entangle such a dangerous enemy in their gaping net. Lured to attend a supposed peace seminar in the commote of Edeirnion in northern Wales, Gruffudd became the victim of a cunning plot engineered by the Norman governance of Chester. Oblivious to the high-level conspiracy, Gruffudd walked into the trap which resulted in his capture and transportation to the hellish confines of a dank cell inside the Norman constructed castle of Chester, where he reportedly languished for a period of twelve years. For the first time since its foundation, the kingdom of Gwynedd was deprived of the stable hand of a royal figurehead, and during Gruffudd's long-term incarceration, the whole of the kingdom lay exposed to the naked aggression of the Normans.

As advocates of terrifying raids, the Norman land grabbers proceeded to write the infamous name of their race across the green pastures of Gwynedd with a seemingly endless shedding of Welsh blood. Hugh d'Avranches, the earl of Chester, secured for himself a collection of forty recognised manors that stretched across the fertile plains of Cheshire and over the threshold of the northern Welsh border. Acting in conjunction with his chosen barons, one of whom held the lordships and manors of Mold and Hawarden, the occupation of northern Wales had begun in earnest. While Gruffudd remained securely under lock and key, whole towns and villages throughout northern Wales were put to the torch during a tempest of violence. The powerful community of Norman barons in the marcher territories then busied themselves with the task of erecting a series of motte and bailey castles along the entire length of the Welsh border, the style of which the inhabitants of Wales had not witnessed before. Using local forests as a plentiful supply of timber, they speedily erected fortifications which were constructed entirely of timber and earth, boasting as its marked centrepiece an earthen mound or 'motte' of up to thirty feet in height. Surrounding the motte was a palisade of timber, a simple, but effective, defensive wall. These revolutionary fortifications served a multitude of uses for their occupiers, including as a base for administration, attack, defence and domination of the surrounding region, which they endeavoured to consolidate and colonise. Within a few years of the battle of Hastings, an arc of frontier castles stared intently towards north-eastern

Tyddyn Mount, some two miles south-east of Mold, is probably a motte and bailey.

Wales, among which were Chester, Shotwick, Pulford, Hawarden, and Dodleston. From their castle bases, the barons of the border began to seize further Welsh lands, commencing a momentous struggle that would endure for 200 years.

Gruffudd ap Cynan's prolonged period of captivity in Chester Castle was ended by an extraordinary stroke of good fortune. A near contemporary account written by Gruffudd's biographer paints a vivid picture of the king's dramatic escape. According to this source, a Welshman from the district of Edeirnion, named Cynwrig Hir, was responsible for the rescue of the royal prisoner. On the day of Gruffydd's escape, the people of Chester were buying goods from the bustling market-place, and while inside the city walls to trade, Cynwrig Hir noticed a manacled figure close to the town centre. Recognising the bedraggled and gaunt figure to be the ruler of Gwynedd, he proceeded to risk his own life by conducting a personal rescue mission. It was the dinner hour in the busy city precincts and Gruffudd ap Cynan's appointed guards were noticeably drunk. Cynwrig single-handedly picked up the greatly weakened Gruffudd and, with remarkable agility, carried him towards the city walls where he concealed him until nightfall. Once the streets became deserted, Cynwrig whisked Gruffudd through a gateway in the walls and, beneath the protective blanket of nightfall, took him to a secret location where he was kept for a number of days. Once the king had regained sufficient strength, he was taken to Anglesey and from there sailed across the Irish Sea to continue his convalescence in the care of his trusted Irish allies.

During the course of Gruffudd ap Cynan's imprisonment, the Normans made monumental strides in their efforts to control the coast of northern Wales. The Welsh cantrefs of Rhos and Rhufoniog were seized by Robert Tillieul (Robert of Rhuddlan) and motte and bailey castles were erected at Deganwy, Caernarfon and Aber Lleiniog. During this period, the castle at Rhuddlan became a pivotal Norman stronghold.

As the Norman successes continued unhindered, men began to enlist with

Gruffudd ap Cynan's cause, thereby increasing his chances of organising a military campaign of his own making, with the intention of smashing the Norman dominance of northern Wales. The flag of revolt was defiantly raised in 1094, and King William II (William Rufus, the son and successor of William the Conqueror) responded by leading two ultimately ineffective campaigns against Gruffudd ap Cynan in 1095 and 1097.

In 1098, Gruffudd ap Cynan recovered Anglesey, and over the course of the next three years he regained western Gwynedd and defeated Hugh, earl of Chester in numerous border skirmishes. Hugh d'Avranches, died in 1101, and this coincided with the resurgence of Gruffudd ap Cynan. From the outset of his reign, the middle-aged Gruffudd devoted the bulk of his energies to the rebuilding of Gwynedd. He introduced a revolutionary programme of internal recovery which flourished for the duration of his reign. Desecrated and abandoned churches were either rebuilt or repaired, and courts for settling disputes and matters of law were introduced. The people of Gwynedd were actively encouraged to embrace a drive toward agricultural reformation, and the unpleasant images of fire-scorched meadows and barren wastes were replaced by the colourful spectacle of fields and fertile acres brimming with crops. Gwynedd prospered during this period of harmony and stability, and during the twilight years of Gruffudd's reign, remained devoid of any prolonged periods of turbulence and warfare.

5

Owain ap Gruffudd ap Cynan ap Iago, or as he is more commonly known to history, Owain Gwynedd, was probably born sometime during the first decade of the twelfth century at the Welsh royal court of Aberffraw on the island of Anglesey. At the time of his birth the royal court (the *llys*) at Aberffraw served as the chief residence of the ruling family of Gwynedd and was the epicentre of the kingdom, being traditionally regarded as its capital. Owain Gwynedd was the second of the three sons of Gruffudd ap Cynan, ruler of Gwynedd, his brothers being Cadwallon (Owain's senior) and Cadwaladr (Owain's junior) and he had at least five sisters, including Gwenllian and Susanna. Through his father, Owain Gwynedd inherited the bloodline of two royal families: his paternal grandfather, Cynan ap Iago, a claimant to the throne of Gwynedd, who after the murder of his father, Iago, in 1039, was forced into exile in Ireland. Cynan ap Iago had married Ragnhildir, the daughter of Olaf Sihtricson, king of the powerful Hiberno-Scandinavian community of Dublin. Owain Gwynedd had also inherited royal blood from his mother's side of the family, being the grandson of Owain ab Edwin (d 1105), a powerful nobleman of northern Wales and a former rival to Gruffudd ap Cynan. Courtesy of a near contemporary biography *Historia Gruffud Vab Kenan,* dedicated to Owain's father, Gruffudd ap Cynan, generations of Welsh historians have been rewarded with a unique insight into the early career of Owain Gwynedd. Included in the text is a commentary charting the meteoric rise of a gifted Welsh warrior intent on forging his own individual name on the turbulent landscape of twelfth-century Wales. His rise to national eminence did not in fact surprise any of his contemporaries; such was the exceptional greatness of his character.

During the year 1114, Henry I, king of England (reigned 1100–35, nicknamed the 'Lion of Justice'), brother and successor of the deceased William II (Rufus, d 1100) and youngest son of William the Conqueror (d 1081), undertook a military campaign against northern Wales. The substantial force of men that he mustered was believed at the time to be the largest land army that had ever been employed by a reigning king of England against Wales. Numerically disadvantaged by a force numbering many thousands of men drawn from across the length and breadth of England, and supported by armed contingents from Scotland, Normandy and Wales itself, Gruffudd ap Cynan, the ruler of Gwynedd, inevitably conceeded to Henry's vast numbers in the field. During this particular campaign, Gruffudd's son, Owain Gwynedd, was too young to have experienced an enemy's advance across the landscape of his native Gwynedd and the gifted soldier that he became was still some years in the future. During the natural onset of old-age, the curse of ill-health had begun to inflict its cruel spell on the tired figure

Aberffraw, Anglesey.
It is difficult to imagine that today's small coastal village in the south-west corner of Anglesey was once the principal seat of the mediaeval rulers of Gwynedd.

of Gruffudd ap Cynan, and weary from the many years spent fighting and campaigning, the king wisely passed on the important function of standard bearers of Gwynedd's war campaigns to his three able-bodied sons Cadwallon, Owain, and Cadwaladr. They did not disappoint their father and in 1124, a force that they had marshalled seized lands in the cantref of Meirionnydd in north-west Wales from rival Welsh nobles. As the power struggle between various Welsh factions continued, the northern cantrefs of Rhos, Rhufoniog and Dyffryn Clwyd fell to Gwynedd in 1125. In 1132, another campaign was launched by Gruffudd's sons, the tentacles of their ambition this time expanding menacingly into the neighbouring Welsh kingdom of Powys. Sometime during the course of this campaign, Cadwallon was killed, and the death of his elder brother elevated Owain Gwynedd to the position of being his father's oldest surviving son.

On the evening of Sunday, 1 December 1135, Henry I drew his last breath, ending his 35-year reign as king of England. Having died in France after falling ill while on a hunting trip, the monarch's sixty-seven year old body was delicately wrapped in ox hides and sprinkled with a generous layer of salt in preparation for the journey across sea to England for burial. Despite fathering an estimated twenty illegitimate children, Henry ended his eventful life without the blessing of a recognised and legitimate male heir. The uncertainty surrounding the succession forced England's barons to assemble to discuss the crisis. In Wales, the unexpected death of such a powerful enemy, presented the native rulers of the various kingdoms an opportunity to dislodge the Anglo-Normans from their power bases in Wales. The prospect of a renewed Welsh revolt was strengthened considerably when a civil war erupted in England between the two rival claimants to the vacant English throne. Henry's daughter, the Empress Matilda, was considered by her supporters in England to be the natural successor, but her claim was unpopular with a powerful group of barons due to her marriage to the Count of Anjou, a region of France viewed as a traditional enemy to both England

and Normandy. Opposing Matilda was Etienne de Blois, the Count of Mortain and Boulogne, or Stephen as he is better known to history. Both candidates for the coveted crown of England were the grandchildren of William the Conqueror and therefore first cousins. From the time of Stephen's official coronation as king of England on 22 December 1135, until the signing of the Treaty of Winchester on 6 November 1153, the two rival factions clashed intermittently during a fruitless civil war which many English historians have labelled as 'the years of anarchy.' The Welsh response to the chaos in England was immediate, as a concerted attempt to forever rid Wales of the hated Anglo-Norman intruders erupted countrywide.

Sometime during the year 1137 Owain, after participating in a war campaign directed against the Anglo-Norman held territories in Ystrad Tywi in south-west Wales, returned to Gwynedd to discover that his aged father was dying. Gruffudd ap Cynan was more than 80 years of age and the old warrior was bed-ridden. Cruelly stripped of his eyesight, he lay consigned to the fate that ultimately befalls even the greatest of men. As Gruffudd approached death, a sombre procession of tearful faces would have filed into the royal bedchamber, which included Dafydd, bishop of Bangor, and Archdeacon Simeon. Also among those dutifully gathered at the bedside were Gruffudd's wife, Angharad, and surviving sons Owain and Cadwaladr. Gruffudd's feeble body was delicately anointed with consecrated oils, and the vigil reached a dramatic climax when the old hero turned his ashen face in the direction of his two sons and with his dying words commanded both of them to be brave and united against the enemies of Gwynedd. He was honourably buried near to the great altar inside the sixth-century-built cathedral in Bangor. Shortly after his death, his remarkable feats as a statesman, warrior and law-maker were recorded in the fabric of *Historia Gruffudd Vab Keenan*, the first extant biography of a Welsh ruler. After his death, an elegy was sung by Meilyr Brydydd (d *c*1137/8), the chief court-poet (*pencerdd*) of the royal household, and a section of the praise lavished elegy

confirmed the triumphant deeds already achieved in battle by Gruffudd's two
surviving sons:

> Owain, despoiler of the Angles, will arise,
>
> The defender of the border will win his enemy's place;
>
> The Powys host see his long lifetime (career)
>
> And readily will fear of him come to the brave.
>
> Cadwaladr, the munificent battle-reaper,
>
> Speedy rider on a white steed, a benefactor on the Calends.
>
> Recurrent is the song that their (Owain and Cadwaladr's) bard sings,
>
> In the battle breach it is they who will overcome.

Despite the immense out-pouring of grief which followed the death of
Gruffudd ap Cynan, it failed to divert his eldest son's attention from
conducting the diminution of Anglo-Norman power in Wales. In 1136, Owain
Gwynedd and his brother conducted two military campaigns in western
Wales. When advancing into Anglo-Norman occupied Ceredigion, they
attacked and captured or destroyed the castles at Aberystwyth, Caerwedros,
Dineirth, Castell Gwallter (Walter's Castle) and Cardigan. Owain's campaign
in west Wales witnessed an unprecedented alliance between the northern
kingdom of Gwynedd and the native rulers from central and southern Wales.
Equally determined to crush the Anglo-Norman hold over Ceredigion, these
willingly joined Owain Gwynedd on campaign and included the forces of
Gruffudd ap Rhys (d 1137) of Deheubarth, Madog ap Idnerth (d 1140) of
Elfael and Maelienydd and Hywel ap Maredudd of Brycheiniog. According to
the Welsh chronicles, the formidable army of allied Welshmen numbered
'about six thousand footsoldiers and two thousand mailed horsemen.' If this
impressive figure is considered to be accurate, then it exceeds the fighting
force of 7,000 infantry and 160 knights raised 150 years later by Prince
Llywelyn ap Gruffudd for the purpose of his ill-fated march to Builth in central
Wales during the winter of 1282.

As the drumbeat of Welsh aggression gathered momentum, so too did the opposition's inevitable response to it and the Anglo-Norman barons of south-west Wales raised a strong army commanded by Stephen (constable of Cardigan Castle), supported by Robert FitzMartin (lord of Cemais), the sons of Gerald (steward of Pembroke) and a Flemish force from the cantref of Rhos in south-west Wales. The Anglo-Norman army marched confidently from Aberteifi (Cardigan) in pursuit and the two armies clashed near the mouth of the river Teifi at the battle of Crûg Mawr, a site some two miles outside Cardigan. When charging on to the battlefield in three organised units, the Welsh soldiery reportedly unleashed a great slaughter against the enemy. According to one account, the Anglo-Normans lost 3,000 soldiers in the battle, and those not killed on the battlefield were forced to undertake a panic-stricken retreat to Cardigan Castle, their numbers being so great that the wooden bridge over the Teifi collapsed beneath the weight of fleeing men and horses. Even the neighbouring churches were set alight, burning alive those cowering inside them. The Welsh victory at Crug Mawr in the autumn of 1136 presented the author of *Brut y Tywysogyon – the Red Book of Hergest* with another opportunity to praise the gallantry of Owain Gwynedd and his brother, Cadwaladr:

> ... the men who were two noble and two generous kings; two dauntless ones; two brave lions; two blessed ones; two eloquent ones; two wise ones; protectors of the churches and their champions; the defenders of the poor; the slayers of the foes ... the safest refuge to all who should flee to them; the men who were pre-eminent in energies of souls and bodies; and jointly upholding in unity the whole kingdom of the Britons.

The Welsh offensive was renewed the following year when Owain Gwynedd again targeted Ceredigion in west Wales. Leaving a trail of blazing ruins in his wake – motte and bailey castles were burned at Ystrad Meurig,

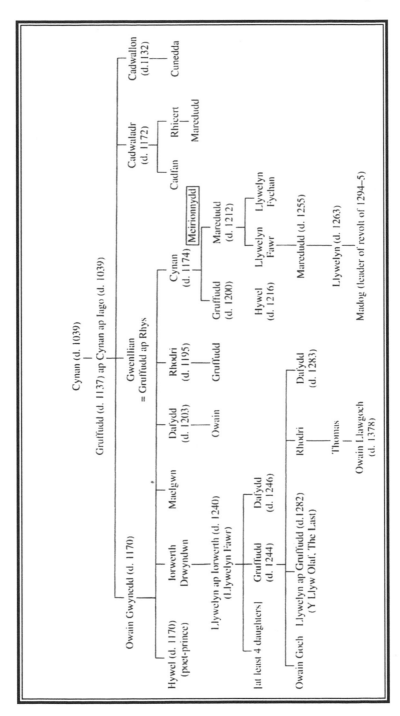

The dynasty of Gwynedd, 1039–1378

Llanstephen and Castle Humphry, and Carmarthen (Caerfyrddin) was captured. The impressive Welsh recovery that had begun the previous year continued, becoming the first major and sustained rebuff to Anglo-Norman expansion in Britain since the Norman Conquest.

Early in 1138, Owain Gwynedd secured military assistance for his next expedition from Ireland, the rulers of Dublin gladly providing him with a fleet of fifteen ships. By land and by sea, the forces of Gwynedd converged upon Cardigan and, joining them on the campaign trail, was a force of allies commanded by Anarawd and Cadell of Deheubarth. Despite failing to capture the castle at Cardigan, Owain still managed to complete the conquest of Ceredigion and confidently annexed the province to the kingdom of Gwynedd. During this turbulent period, Owain's sister, Gwenllian, wife to Gruffudd ap Rhys of the royal house of Deheubarth, died in a battle at Cydweli (Kidwelly) in 1136 whilst bravely leading a Welsh army against a strong force of Anglo-Normans.

Sadly, a contemporary description of Owain's physical appearance has not

Castell Gwallter (Walter's Castle), Llandre, Ceredigion.
Between 1136 and 1138, Owain Gwynedd conducted an insurgency against the
powerful Anglo-Normans in west Wales. Castell Gwallter was captured in 1136.

Dinerth Castle, near Aberarth, Ceredigion
Built around 1110, this was burned by Owain Gwynedd in 1136. The site, which covers about three acres, occupies a strategic hill at the confluence of the river Arth and the Erthyg brook, with steep ravines on three sides.

Caerwedros Castle, near New Quay, Ceredigion.
This display board illustrates how the castle, which is now an unremarkable mound of earth on the west side of the village, would have looked before it was destroyed by Owain Gwynedd in 1136.

Owain Gwynedd
A statue displayed in Caernarfon Castle.

withstood the ages. Nevertheless, we do know that both his parents were described by a contemporary source as being fair or flaxen haired, strong of limb and of healthy complexion. In addition to their physical appearances, Owain's parents were jointly credited by the same source as being eloquent in their everyday speech; his father in particular was proficient in several languages. Based on this evidence, we can confidently speculate that Owain was also similarly proficient in more than one language; perhaps Latin and an understanding of French or even Irish Gaelic shadowing his native Welsh tongue. During his journey to manhood, the young prince would have undergone a laborious training programme that covered the important disciplines of armed combat and general warfare. Trained to master the sword, the spear and the dagger with deathly precision, the youthful Owain would also have been drip-fed a constant diet of war stories, war poems and war songs. Furthermore, as part of his rigorous military tuition, the skills required for good horsemanship would also have been learned, so too the procedure for slaying an enemy at close quarters. Moreover, Owain's important participation on his father's annual war campaigns duly transformed what would have been a fresh-faced youth into a wholly competent adult warrior, whose renowned fighting spirit during the course of what proved to be a lengthy military career never once diminished.

In common with other Welsh rulers of the period, Owain was a seasoned adulterer, enjoying countless relationships with a multitude of women. As a result of so many intimate liaisons, it was rumoured that he may have fathered twenty or more children. Notwithstanding this lustful appetite, Owain committed himself to marriage on two occasions. His first wife was Gwladus, a daughter of Llywarch ap Trahaearn (d c1124), the powerful ruler of Cedewain in central Wales, a matrimonial union perhaps forged to seal a crucial alliance between the royal house of Gwynedd and a native dynasty of central Wales. The marriage is believed to have produced as many as ten children – eight sons (the most prominent being Iorwerth and Maelgwn) and two daughters. Sometime during the early 1130s, Owain married for a second time, to Cristin, the daughter of Goronwy ab Owain (d 1125), an ambitious Welsh nobleman of north-east Wales, which secured another important alliance for the royal house of Gwynedd. The newlyweds were first cousins (Cristin's father, Goronwy and Owain's mother, Angharad being brother and sister), but prior to the marriage, their respective families were dynastic rivals engaged in a bloody power struggle in northern Wales. Ultimately, the union between Owain and Cristin proved successful and produced at least two sons, Dafydd and Rhodri, and at least one daughter. Another prominent son reared from Owain's copious nest of royal offspring was Hywel, a possible heir-designate who had been illegitimately conceived during Owain's earlier liaisons with an Irish woman named Pyfog. Moreover, there is every possibility that Cynan, another of Owain's prominent sons, could also have been the product of another relationship with an unnamed Irish woman. In essence, Owain's amorous adventuring would later prove costly to the well-being of the royal house of Gwynedd when, immediately after Owain's death, a number of his sons battled one another for control of the kingdom during a struggle for power that would take three decades to resolve.

From the year 1140 onwards, Owain Gwynedd appeared to wage open warfare against every opponent imaginable. When seeking to expand the frontiers of his own Gwynedd kingdom, he strenuously locked horns with numerous opponents, including the Anglo-Norman lords of the marches, neighbouring Welsh rulers and even his own brother, Cadwaladr. Wales, during this period, was a collection of kingdoms and satellite kingdoms, the three strongest being Gwynedd in the north-west of Wales, Powys in central Wales and Deheubarth in the south-west of Wales. The military alliance between Owain Gwynedd and the kingdom of Deheubarth had thus far proved instrumental in yielding so many of Owain's successes that had helped to retard the attempted Normanisation of twelfth-century Wales. However, the strong military bond between the two native royal houses came perilously close to breaking point in 1143 after the murder of Anarawd ap Gruffudd, the principal ruler of Deheubarth, a shocking death believed to have been perpetrated by Owain Gwynedd's independently minded and ambitious brother, Cadwaladr. In order to divert the unwanted scourge of a highly damaging civil war, Owain skilfully engaged every ounce of his renowned flair for diplomacy in order to prevent a fruitless conflict between north and south. Furthermore, the ever determined Owain responded to the crisis by launching a campaign of aggression against his disgraced brother. During the turbulent course of what proved to be an alarming fall from grace, the

Cynfael Castle, near Tywyn, Gwynedd
The property of Owain's brother, Cadwaladr, this was set ablaze by Hywel
and Cynan in 1147.

condemned Cadwaladr was fervently harried from Gwynedd, being forced to flee from one bolt hole to another. In 1143, Cadwaladr's castle at Aberystwyth was consigned to the torch by a force commanded by two of Owain's sons, Hywel and Cynan. In 1147, another violent raid was aimed against the tormented Cadwaladr. On this occasion, his newly constructed castle of Cynfal, near Tywyn, was assaulted by Hywel and Cynan, forcing him to abandon another burning fortification. Built on the top of a ridge overlooking the Dysynni estuary, the black plumes of smoke emanating from the keep that reportedly crashed to the floor must have been observed from many miles away. In 1150, hostilities again erupted, resulting in the capture of Cadwaladr's castle at Llanrhystud, near Aberaeron after a siege supervised by Owain Gwynedd's son, Hywel. Finally, in 1152, after almost ten years of conflict between the brothers, Owain forcibly removed Cadwaladr from the comfort of his final refuge, an enclosure on the island of Anglesey. Faced with little alternative, the harassed Cadwaladr fled into exile for a period of five years. Choosing England as his safe haven, he was warmly welcomed by its ruling royal house. A short time after the coronation of Henry II, Cadwaladr was provided with an estate at Ness in Shropshire, and by harbouring the disinherited Cadwaladr, King Henry gained control of a useful political pawn.

The defining thunder of Owain Gwynedd's vigorous pursuit of a mightier Gwynedd echoed loudly throughout the length and breadth of Wales. Sometime around the year 1146, the hilltop castle at Mold fell to Owain's forces, forcing the local Anglo-Norman lord to abandon his lordship. During this same eventful period, the commote of Iâl (Yale) in northern Powys was annexed to Gwynedd by force of arms, resulting in the construction of a fortress in the territory, this being more than likely the motte and bailey castle near Llandegla, later christened Tomen-y-Rhodwydd.

In a determined response to Owain's numerous land gains, a large allied army was assembled by Ranulph II, earl of Chester (d 1153) and Madog ap Maredudd (d 1160), the threatened ruler of Powys. The armies clashed at the

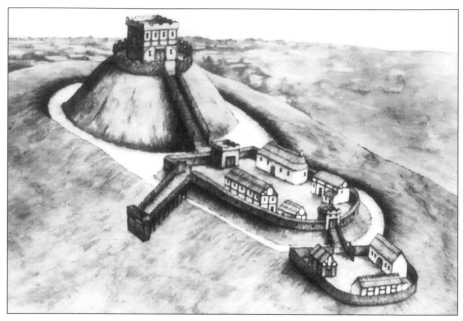

An artist's impression of Mold Castle, Flintshire
This was captured by Owain Gwynedd in c.1146.The motte still survives overlooking Mold
High Street.

pass of Cwnsyllt (Coleshill) in Tegeingl, resulting in another notable victory
for the so far undefeated Owain Gwynedd. The troops from Cheshire were
reportedly cut to pieces and the bulk of the Powysian army fled the battlefield
in abject disarray. Owain's emphatic triumph sent shockwaves across the
border, thereby further boosting his growing aura of invincibility. During this
lively phase of his career, the ruler of Gwynedd drove the Anglo-Normans
from the precincts of Ceredigion in west Wales, forcibly expelled his
troublesome brother from Gwynedd and regained a considerable portion –
if not all – of the strategically important border district of Tegeingl. Owain's
remarkable progress in the field had physically transported him to within
striking distance of the gates of Chester, where from the established position
of his eastern outposts he could stare menacingly towards the historic
riverside citadel once governed by the Romans, but now firmly held in the

mailed fists of the Anglo-Normans. During this harvest of success, there appeared to be only the one set back militarily – the erosion of his territories in Ceredigion held by his son, Hywel, whose power base there had been gradually reduced to nothing during the 1151–3 period as a consequence of the actions of the emerging Rhys ap Gruffudd (The Lord Rhys, d 1197), the sublimely gifted ruler of the royal house of Deheubarth. And so began the dangerous process of a cold war between the once allied native kingdoms of Gwynedd and Deheubarth. This delicate situation endured for more than a decade before an alliance of the powers was resumed in 1165. The question 'Who could realistically mount a serious challenge against the exceptionally gifted Owain Gwynedd?' remained unanswered. But, around the very next corner of Owain's career, there emerged the most powerful challenge yet to his seemingly unstoppable advance, a steely individual who was resolutely determined on reducing the wild flames of revolt into a heap of smoking ashes.

Tomen-y-Rhodwydd, Llandegla, Denbighshire
One of the finest surviving earthwork castles in Wales, it is probably the
'castle in Iâl' built by Owain in 1149.

6

From the occasion of his glittering coronation ceremony at Westminster Abbey on 22 December 1135, to the moment of his peaceful death at Dover in Kent on 25 October 1154, King Stephen ruled the kingdom of England. His lacklustre reign of 19 years was dominated by the turbulence of a lengthy and damaging civil war. Notwithstanding the initial revolt of Stephen's enemies and the later defection of a number of the country's leading barons who swarmed to the opposing corner of his cousin and rival claimant, the heiress Matilda (d 1167), Stephen somehow managed to cling to power during the episodic hostilities, even suffering the humiliation of capture and an eight month period of imprisonment in 1141. Stephen's fragile realm suffered another blow when the lands to the north of the Ribble and Tyne were overrun by rampaging Scottish armies, resulting in King David I of Scotland (d 1153), a close supporter of Matilda, establishing his capital at Carlisle. On 6 November 1153, the civil war in England was finally brought to a satisfactory climax by the signing of a peace treaty at Winchester. It was agreed by both parties that Stephen would remain king for the remainder of his natural life, while Henry FitzEmpress, the eldest of the three sons of Matilda, was acknowledged by all as the nominated successor.

Exhausted by two decades of civil war that had severely blighted his reign, Stephen's troubled life finally ended in peace. After receiving official word of Stephen's death, the 21-year-old Henry, together with his wife, Eleanor of Aquitaine, and their one-year-old child, William, sailed from France to collect the coveted prize of his promised inheritance. On 19 December 1154, he was

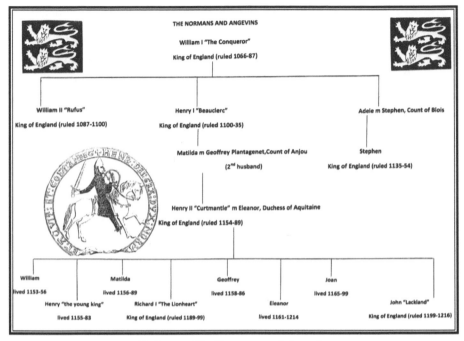

Pedigree of the Normans and Angevins

crowned as *Henri II, Roi de L'Angleterre* (Henry II, King of England) at Westminster Abbey. The French language title was unquestionably more familiar to a man whose knowledge of the English language was thought to be non-existent, historians believing that during the course of Henry's lifetime not even a single syllable of the English tongue passed from his lips.

Henry, the son of Geoffrey, count of Anjou (d 1151) and the Empress Matilda, was born at Le Mans in the French territory of Anjou on 5 March 1133. At the time of his accession to the throne of England, he was also count of Maine, duke of Normandy, count of Anjou and duke of Aquitaine, and he became England's first Angevin (or Plantagenet) king at the head of a vast empire which would last for 50 years in Normandy and Anjou, 299 years in Aquitaine and 331 years in England.

Charter of Henry II addressed generally (19 December 1154):

King Henry II
A statue displayed in
Caernarfon Castle.

Henry (by the grace of God), king of the English, duke of the men of Normandy and Aquitaine, and count of the Angevins to all his earls, barons and liegemen, both French and English, greeting. Know that for the honour of God and holy Church, and for the common restoration of my whole realm, I have granted and restored, and by this present charter confirmed, to God and to the holy Church, and to all my earls, barons and vassals all concessions, gifts, liberties and free customs, which King Henry, my grandfather, granted and conceded to them. Likewise all evil customs, which he abolished and relaxed, I also grant to be relaxed and abolished in my name and in that of my heirs. Wherefore I will, and firmly command, that holy Church and all my earls, barons and vassals shall have and hold all these customs, gifts, liberties and freedom from pecuniary exactions, freely and unmolested, fully, rightly and in peace from me and my heirs for themselves and their heirs, as freely and peaceably and fully in everything as King Henry, my grandfather, granted and conceded to them and confirmed by his charter.

Witness: Richard of Luce.

At Westminster.

Excited by the dawning of a new era, a number of contemporary scribes rejoiced at Henry's coming to power. Henry of Huntingdon (d *c*1156) wrote:

> England, long numbed by mortal chill,
>
> you now grow warm, revived by the heat of a new sun.
>
> You lift the country's bowed head,
>
> and wiping away the tears of sorrow, you weep for joy.
>
> with tears, you utter these words to your foster child:

"You are spirit, I am flesh:

now as you enter I am restored to life."

Within the precincts of Peterborough Abbey, an English monk recorded the news of Henry's landing on the shores of England by inking the following words inside *The Anglo-Saxon Chronicle*

1154. The earl (Henry Fitz Empress) was beyond the sea, but no man dared do other than good through great awe of him. Then when he came to England, he was received with great honour and was consecrated as king in London on the Sunday before mid-winter day, and there held a great court.

In actual fact, Henry was regarded as a foreigner in the lands of his new kingdom, and during this period of history England was more comprehensively involved in Continental affairs than at any time before or since. As Frenchmen, the Norman and Plantagenet kings of England never completely forgot their French roots. Although the island of Britain escaped direct Continental rule, the imposing shadow of France lay across it for the best part of 400 years. In order to govern England successfully, Henry's primary objectives at the beginning of his reign were to recover for the Crown the royal castles lost and to visibly crush all resistance to his name. Initially, two prominent Marcher nobles, Roger of Hereford and Hugh de Mortimer, steadfastly refused to conform to Henry's rule and both vowed to rebel. However, by the summer of 1155, the rebel-held castles of Gloucester, Cleobury, Wigmore and Bridgnorth had all surrendered to the superior power of the new king. During this period of transition, Henry saw fit to order the expulsion of a large number of Flemish marauders from the kingdom, instructing them to leave *en masse* by an appointed date.

7

Beginning his reign with characteristic energy and enthusiasm, Henry II achieved his primary objectives. The realm was no longer tainted by war, law and order was restored and the party of temperamental barons bent a compliant knee to their new sovereign. In addition, the duchy of Brittany, the one remaining independent territory in western France, came a step closer to becoming another of Henry's provinces when in 1156, Henry's brother, Geoffrey d'Anjou, was installed at Nantes as count of Lower Brittany. However, only a short distance away from Henry's English realm there remained the assertive figure of Owain, ruler of Gwynedd, whose menacing progress remained unchecked. On 16 December 1153, Ranulph II, the powerful earl of Chester, died unexpectedly, leaving behind a son Hugh who was a minor and not yet ready to ascend to his father's position. The news of the death of such a powerful Anglo-Norman of the northern March was warmly received by the fiercely ambitious Owain whose own forces had recently gained a foothold in the north-east Wales cantref of Tegeingl, the eastern fringes of which overlooked the border city of Chester. During Stephen's chaotic reign, the Welsh military renaissance had been allowed to flourish unmolested, a theme that betrayed English royal policy. From the Norman victory at Hastings in 1066 to the Edwardian Conquest of Wales two centuries later, Stephen and Richard (The Lionheart, reigned 1189–99) were the only two kings of England, from a group of nine, who did not personally undertake a military expedition into Wales. In Richard's case, he may be excused of any accusations of a disinterest in a Welsh policy as during his ten-year reign he

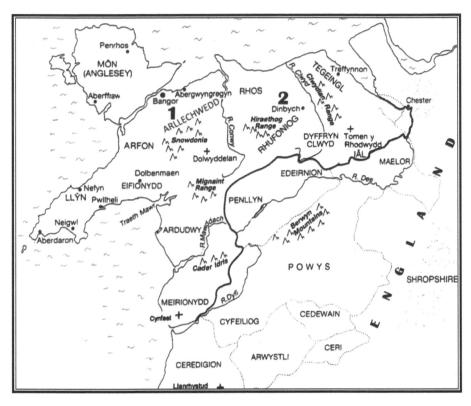

The extent of the Kingdom of Gwynedd c.1170

――――― The boundaries of Gwynedd

·········· Other regional boundaries

ʌ   Mountain ranges

+   Castles built or rebuilt by the
     Gwynedd dynasty

●   Religious centres associated
     with the dynasty

1   Gwynedd uwch Conwy

2   Gwynedd is Conwy,
     alias Perfeddwlad
     alias the Four Cantrefs

spent less than six months in his English kingdom. In contrast to Stephen's traditional image as a weak sovereign, Henry Plantagenet was portrayed as an individual of great determination and one chiselled from a far sturdier material, choosing to personally lead a military campaign against Wales, the first royal expedition against a native ruler since the reign of Henry I, some 36 years earlier.

During the course of world history, there have been a great many individuals who were revered as inspirational leaders, a particularly productive era proving to be the middle to latter years of the twelfth century. The remarkable talents who lived during this particular era were genuinely gifted and their exploits resonate to this day. Genghis Khan (d.c. 1227) , Saladin (d. 1193) and Frederick I Barbarossa (d.1190). Similarly, in the eyes of many British historians, the twelfth-century figures of Henry II and Owain Gwynedd are justly accredited with great praise.

> The history of the English people would have been a great and noble history whatever king had ruled over the land seven hundred years ago. But the history as we know it, and the mode of government which has actually grown up among us is in fact due to the genius of the great king (Henry) whose will England was guided from 1154 to 1189. [*Henry the Second*, J. R. Green]

> In Henry the Second the English had a king of outstanding abilities. Short and strongly built, he was famous for his phenomenal energy, both of body and mind. Only a man of Henry's talents could have administered so large an empire with any degree of success.[*The Monarchs of Britain*, Josephine Ross]

> Henry's empire stretched from the Arctic Ocean to the Pyrenees. Few mortals have led so full a life as Henry or have drunk so deeply of the cups of triumph and sorrow. [*A History of The English Speaking Peoples*, Winston Churchill]

> Henry the Second is widely regarded as one of England's greatest monarchs. A dynamic ruler, able in mind and body, he was an energetic, powerful, sometimes

volatile ruler. A successful warrior-king in his earlier years, his reign was also notable for the development of English common law, with many processes being established. [*Kings and Queens*, Paul Cheshire, General Editor, Professor David Loades]

If Gruffudd ap Cynan was the hero of Welsh defensive warfare, Owain (Gwynedd) was the hero of victory. The greatest Welsh figure of the middle of the 12th century is certainly Owain Gwynedd. [*The Age of Owain Gwynedd*, Paul Barbier]

It is for his leadership and prudence in the struggle with Henry, a man of very different mould from (King) Stephen and one of the most powerful kings of his day, that we must award Owain (Gwynedd) the eminent position which is admittedly his in the history of his country. [*Wales. Her Origins, Struggles and Later History Institutions and Manners*, G. Stone]

It may be argued that Owain [Gwynedd] is the greatest of the four great men who stand supreme in the history of our nation (between the years 1137–1282). When Owain succeeded his father in 1137, he had already demonstrated over the years his efficiency, energy, courage and wisdom. He continued to reveal the same virtues for thirty-three more years. *[Land of My Fathers*, Gwynfor Evans]

It was in fact, under him [Owain Gwynedd] that the Welsh nation attained the full measure of national consciousness which enabled it for a century and a half to successfully resist absorption into the English realm. [*A History of Wales*, J. E. Lloyd]

In the new year of 1156, Eleanor of Aquitaine gave birth to Matilda, and during that same year, Henry and Eleanor's much cherished three-year-old son, William, count of Poitiers, tragically died at the royal castle of Wallingford on the river Thames. The infant was buried at the feet of his great grandfather, King Henry I (d 1135), in the nearby abbey of Reading. At the end of that emotion charged year, Henry and his consort spent the Christmas season together in Bordeaux, in the province of Aquitaine in southern France. More than ten years older than her husband, Eleanor was considered to be one of the richest women in Europe and had brought Aquitaine under English control by her marriage to Henry in 1152. Two more strongly-minded, forceful and determined people could hardly have been imagined. Eleanor was beautiful, wanton, capricious, sophisticated, highly intelligent and accustomed to having her own way. During that Christmas season in southern France, she fell pregnant again with a son who was born at the King's House in Beaumont Palace, Oxfordshire, on 8 September 1157, and named Richard, who would become known to history as Richard Coeur de Lion (the Lionheart).

On or around 8 April 1157, King Henry returned to England. At Whitsun, he was at Bury St Edmunds for the purpose of a ceremonial crown wearing, and on 17 July held a royal council at Northampton, and in all probability it was during this sitting that the detailed plans for a military campaign against Owain Gwynedd were finalised. The critical moment for Henry had arrived. Unrestrained by other matters, he could focus his entire energy on resolving the problem of Wales, a country which he had yet to molest. On the eve of the campaign in northern Wales, it appeared that the odds were overwhelmingly stacked in Henry's favour. The threat from Scotland had evaporated by virtue of its king, the 16-year-old Malcolm IV (Malcolm the Maiden, d 9 December 1165), compliantly signing the Treaty of Chester and, by doing so, the Scottish claim on Cumberland, Westmorland and Northumbria was renounced. From that moment onwards, the Anglo-Scottish border would be permanently fixed on the Solway and the Tweed. The situation in Ireland was not yet considered critical enough for the activation of any form of royal campaign. In England, the early phase of Henry's reign had successfully brought to heel those rebellious barons whose power bases had grown dangerously strong during the civil war. In Wales, Henry was not short of powerful allies, as a small but prominent group of Welsh rulers braced themselves for a war against their feared adversary Owain Gwynedd. Hence, the massed ranks of Henry's invasion force would consist of armed Welshmen that included Cadwaladr ap Gruffudd (the exiled brother of Owain Gwynedd), Madog ap Maredudd (the ruler of the large kingdom of Powys and brother-in-law to Owain Gwynedd by virtue of his marriage to Owain's sister, Susanna), Iorweth Goch (the highly ambitious younger brother of Madog ap Maredudd) and Hywel ab Ieuaf of central Wales (who was known to style himself in written correspondences as *Rex Arguestli*, the king of Arwystli). If the rising power of Owain Gwynedd was to be suffocated militarily and his kingdom politically controlled, Henry needed to prepare his campaign wisely, and in this crucial endeavour the tireless Henry could not in any way be faulted.

As England prepared for a summer war, the national call to arms induced a frenzy of activity across the country; the baron in his castle, the lord on his manor, the inhabitants of the towns, the commoners on their small holdings, each received word of their duty bound obligation to the overlord. Known as feudalism – the established system by which land was held in return for service and homage to a superior lord – they, as Henry's subjects, were duty bound by its rules. The men provided under the terms of the feudal levy owed their allegiance in a practical sense to their immediate lord, although the king was still to be regarded as the ultimate commander-in-chief of the army as a whole. Every able-bodied man between the age of 15 and 60 was expected to adhere to this system and the period of an individual's military service to his overlord was usually forty days each year. With a population of around 2.5 million, England's well-oiled military machine could effectively churn out vast numbers of fighting men. We do not know precisely how many men formed Henry's royal army of 1157, but the '30,000 men' quoted by one source is most probably an exaggeration.

In 1157, King Henry II had an accurate idea of the size of the force that he could reliably muster and what the composition of its ranks would be. The full scale of feudal service at that time amounted in theory to some 5,000 knights, an impressive number by any standards. For the campaign against Owain Gwynedd, a special levy was raised that focussed on a much longer term of service instead of mere numbers, and by Henry demanding a third of his knightly number, the customary forty days service was extended. As the royal writs were distributed, so began an enormous enterprise to accumulate adequate provisions for the royal army. A plentiful supply of food would be required, so too, a mass of blankets, tents, tools and weaponry. It has been estimated that an army of 10,000 men would need around 1,500 quarters of grain each week. During the preparations for Henry's 1165 follow-up campaign in northern Wales, the Pipe Rolls reveal that corn for the campaign was provided by the English counties of Gloucestershire, Lincolnshire, Oxfordshire, Berkshire and Worcestershire, with malt, oats, beans, peas, bacons and cheeses being among the commodities collected for the royal army. Similar details can be extracted from the Pipe Rolls for the provision of foodstuffs for Henry's later expedition to Ireland. Over 6,424 measures (probably quarters) of wheat, 2,000 of oats, 584 of beans, with 4,106 bacon pigs and 160 quarters of salt were provided. As the food was transported alongside the marching army, special measures were applied to prevent its deterioration. Flour was placed into good strong clean casks, closely packed and pressed down, with a few sticks of hazel and a handful of salt at the bottom of each vessel to prevent the contents turning bad. When grain was stored, it had to be turned regularly to prevent it becoming damp and rotten. Of course, there were numerous ways in which mediaeval armies could be supplied with such victuals. The Crown could make elaborate arrangements to supply victuals, using all the resources of local officials to collect the goods which were then transported to the campaign base. Similarly, the wealthy local magnates could be expected to take their own supplies with them. Moreover, an advancing army on foreign soil in desperate need of nourishment might well succeed in feeding itself by foraging the local land or stealing from its inhabitants. The king also appealed to abbeys in his realm, specifically requesting their aid to provide him with a large number of carts to transport his tents and other goods along the war trail. Furthermore, supplies of linen bandages, ointments, various potions and medicines would be held by the army's surgeons, a group of injury specialists whose presence on campaign was essential. Likewise, huge numbers of horses, specifically bred for the routine toughness of war, would accompany the royal army. In addition, ships selected for the king's fleet would need to be serviced, repaired and adequately stocked. The mobilisation of such a huge task force would understandably take time, organisation and money.

A mediaeval 'barber-surgeon' as portrayed by a modern re-enactor.

The colossal enterprise that represented Henry's campaign predictably involved a significant outlay of funds. It has been estimated that his 1165 invasion of northern Wales cost in the region of an incredible £7,500, a vast sum of money considering that in 1130, during the reign of Henry I, the total of the king's revenue audited at the Exchequer was £24,500. For the later expedition to Ireland in 1171, when the Crown required its officers to supply the royal army with horses, they were instructed to pay the going rate of 40s (£2) per steed. Good quality horses were extremely valuable and the value and standard of each could vary considerably. Early in the reign of Henry's great-great-grandson, Edward II (1307–27), a total of fifteen tents were purchased for the king and his campaigning army at a cost of £500. The sources clearly confirm that England's kings spent money on a grand scale, on war especially, but also on buildings, retainers, food and drink, clothing and jewellery. This extravagant campaign of spending required huge revenue to fund it. The four crucial components of this revenue were the Crown lands (or royal demesne), income obtained from feudal overlordship, taxes and the vast sums derived from justice. During this period of history, London was viewed as one of the wealthiest metropolises of the western world. Being the largest city in the British Isles, and firmly established as the political, economic and administrative capital of the kingdom, and the country's major port, importers brought to it gold, spices, frankincense from Arabia and precious stones from the Nile. In addition, purple fabrics came from the East Indies, oil of palm from Babylon, arms from Scythia and barrels of wine from France. In the city alone, there was an estimated population of 40,000, an established 126 churches, and 3 colleges that taught grammar, poetry and rhetoric. Henry's capital was crowded, polluted and noisy, with the sound of bells, street cries and the bellowing of driven livestock reverberating through its streets. And, at the heart of this colourful paradise of riches lay its principal citizen, the king. Henry's plenitude of wealth was not solely confined to London as his royal lands were to be found in virtually every county in the kingdom. At his manor house at Woodstock near Oxford, Henry indulged his hobby of keeping exotic animals given to him as gifts by foreign leaders. When founding the first royal menagerie, the rare sight of lions, leopards, lynxes, camels and even a porcupine wandering the royal parkland consumed the attention of all visitors. During the period of Henry's reign, the Crown owned at least sixty castles and an impressive collection of fine hunting lodges. The king's personal portfolio of properties included residences at Feckenham, near Worcester, Kinver in Staffordshire, Guildford in Surrey, Clarendon Palace in Wiltshire, and Geddington in Northamptonshire. Amongst his raft of impressive castles were those built at Nottingham, Gloucester, Winchester, Marlborough and Ludgershall. Of the chief royal residences of Henry's day, incredibly three are still in use to this day: the Palace of Westminster, the Tower of London and Windsor Castle. Even Louis VII, the king of France (reigned 1137–80), enviously informed Walter Map (d. *c.*1210), a clerk and important member of Henry's household, 'Your king, the lord of England, has men and horses, gold and silk and jewels and fruits, game and everything else while we in France have nothing but bread and wine and gaiety.'

During the summer season of 1157, the city of Chester was pulsating with activity. Mediaeval Chester boasted many landmarks of architectural brilliance, including the crumbling remains of a Roman amphitheatre, an imposing castle and the impressive stone-built churches of St John and St Werburgh. Home to a bustling market and a thriving sea port, a daily crowd of visitors swept noisily through the labyrinth of ancient streets – brewers, beggars and thieves, clergymen and masons, and soldiers and a multitude of traders. Tattered wagons laden with goods inched their way through the narrow streets as people carrying baskets packed with eggs, butter and a selection of Cheshire's finest cheeses breezed past the local midden, seemingly oblivious to the stench emanating from the waste methodically cast there by the community of local butchers. But, by the end of that summer season of 1157, the city's carefree ambience would be derailed by the drumbeat of an unwanted war, as two red-blooded warriors from afar resolutely led their iron-clad armies towards the shores of the Dee.

Sometime during the final quarter of July, 1157, the majestic figure that was Henry II swept into the border city of Chester, at the head of his *Familia Regis*, a body of heavily-armed men more commonly known as the royal bodyguard or household troop. Henry brought to the historic walled city a powerful force of well-trained, well-equipped and highly disciplined soldiers, composed of knights, squires and sergeants. The king's personal household formed the core of the royal army and were justly regarded as the elite troops of their day. Its commanders were men of great power and wealth and enjoyed an intimate relationship with the king. During times of peace, its officers served as sheriffs, justices, ambassadors or other important royal agents. To accommodate and pay for the *Familia*, Henry routinely billeted them in his castles so that they earned their keep even in times of peace, a policy that demanded absolute loyalty to the sovereign. When these mounted horsemen swept into Chester, they would have formed an impressive spectacle to all those witnessing the rare sighting of a ruling monarch accompanied by his personal entourage. Riding almost knee to knee, astride magnificent warhorses, the clattering procession of mailed knights sat tall and straight-legged in their saddles, whilst hanging down from the pommels of their saddles, their helmets shone a brilliant white, courtesy of the trusted process of scouring with sand, vinegar and wire. The Earl of Essex, the king's standard bearer by hereditary right, rode next to the king and held Henry's royal banner aloft for all to see. It was a long flag with pointed tails, a blood-red ripple of precious silk adorned with the two golden lions of Normandy. A majority of the knights who accompanied the king were served by a squire who usually rode behind his master on a spare warhorse whilst carrying upright the owner's long ash lance. Of course, the genuine pride of a knight's personal armoury was his sword, so beloved by the wielder that they were often named by them. Manufactured by the hand of a proficient blacksmith, the blade could measure anything between 30 and 40 inches in length, some 2 to 3 inches wide and averaging around 4 pounds in weight. These elite fighting men were the supreme masters of the battlefield, conditioned to withstand the rigorous demands and hardships associated with the blood and thunder of mediaeval warfare.

Henry calculatingly chose the city of Chester as the point of muster for his army of invasion. The decision was flawless. Chester is a typical garrison town, formidably walled all round, and by the time of Henry's arrival during the summer of 1157, the old Roman walls had been extended to the west and the south to form a complete circuit of defences measuring about two miles in circumference. The historic settlement is situated upon the eastern bank of the Dee river, about twenty miles from the swell of the Irish Sea, and every chapter of Chester's history appears etched into the very fabric of the city. It is a place where Roman soldiers marched to war, Viking raiders wreaked havoc, and Norman invaders conquered the Anglo-Saxons. During the first century AD, a Roman legion had almost certainly established a wooden fortress at Chester, a place they had christened as Deva. Upon completion, the Roman garrison there absorbed an area of over 60 acres and was regarded as the largest of the Roman fortresses in Britain. Standing sentinel against the threat of attack from the surrounding indigenous tribes, Roman Chester settled competently into the role of an important military settlement and a principal route centre. Major Roman roads connected Deva (Chester) with parts of northern Britain, south-eastern Britain and the borderlands of Wales, and the arteries of the minor roadways branched off into north Wales and many parts of Cheshire. Long after the Romans had withdrawn from Britain, a large number of their roads remained in the use of the native inhabitants, including the established route from Chester into the interior of north-east Wales.

When Henry II rode into Chester at the head of his impressive household troop, the reception he received from its citizens would undoubtedly have been more cordial than the one given to the army of his ancestor, William the Conqueror, on the occasion of a royal visitation to the city a century earlier. During the winter of 1069/70, Chester came under attack during an infamous period of William I's reign, the so-called 'Harrying of the North.' Thanks to the vindictive hand of a Norman army schooled in brutality, the city suffered extensive fire damage, with up to 200 dwellings deliberately torched. Under Norman rule, Chester had been rebuilt by the end of the eleventh century, a weir established across the Dee, watermills constructed on each bank to process grain to flour, and a motte and bailey castle built to serve the newly established earl and to act as the hub of the entire earldom.

Henry held a royal council at Northampton on 17 July 1157, and there is a tendency to suggest that he may already have been negotiating his journey northwards to Chester. Assuming that he journeyed overland, the physical demands of undertaking such a taxing exercise would perhaps have caused a number of lesser beings to wilt, but not Henry, a man who was renowned throughout the kingdom for his endless reserves of energy. On his arrival at his quarters inside Chester's walls, a small number of the king's Cheshire subjects would have been able to fix an inquisitive eye upon the physical figure of their supreme overlord. There, stood before them, was King Henry II, his glittering trophy cabinet of titles included – duke of Normandy, count of Anjou, duke of Aquitaine, count of Maine, and in 1171, lord of Ireland. His courtiers and personal retainers knew him by another name Curtmantle (*Courtmanteau*), so-called because of Henry's fondness for wearing the distinctive, short Angevin cape which hung on his shoulders, and marked him out amidst the Anglo-Norman knights, with their long fur-lined cloaks hanging freely to the ground. The king was a powerfully built man, slightly above medium height and blessed with sound limbs, a broad square chest, muscular arms and a short bull-like neck. He had inherited the red hair of his father, Geoffrey Plantagenet, and a freckled complexion to match. Contemporary authorities describe his face as fiery and lion-like. The focal point of his head, which was round and well proportioned, were his grey-coloured eyes, full of expression, but rather prominent, and sometimes bloodshot. The king's muscular legs were visibly bowed from the activity of incessant riding, a skill which he had mastered during his youth. His unusual and distinctive voice was harsh and high-pitched and frequently cracked during customary bouts of temper, a trait he had inherited from his ancestors. Sometimes, when in the depths of his infamous rages, he would throw himself to the floor and the drama would continue by him rolling around, but nobody at court would be foolish enough to laugh at such a ludicrous sight.

Though not regarded as handsome, Henry was conscious of his personal appearance. The king possessed two grave fears: baldness and obesity. To combat these life-long anxieties, he always kept the style of his hair closely cropped and he exercised at every given opportunity. Henry was renowned for his phenomenal energy. He never sat except at meals or on horseback, and he transacted all business standing. Even when his own feet and legs were covered with sores from incessant exertion, he remained walking or standing till after nightfall. He was industrious, restless, fixed in purpose and a brilliant organiser. Wonderfully rapid in execution, he was an adroit and formidable man-at-arms. In physical capacity he was considered by observers to be second to none, incapable of no activity which another could perform. He heard mass daily and during the most solemn part of the service was constantly whispering to his courtiers, or scribbling, or looking at pictures. The power of this human dynamo never seemed to diminish, he was constantly on the move, progressing methodically round every corner of his realm on horseback, delivering justice, gathering taxes and bringing the barons to order. These tasks he achieved in the company of his entire court who shared his constant journeying. In 1170 alone, he accomplished a total land mileage of 2,050 miles, which equated to 5.75 miles per day. He was eloquent, affable and jocose, so persuasive in manner that few could fail to be charmed by his presentation. He had an amazing memory, well stocked with the lessons of past times, and never forgot a face.

Akin to all other beings, there were obvious weaknesses to the king's character. He displayed no mercy whatsoever to his household which accompanied him on his regular treks. The arduous journeys by rough trackways through the kingdom's fenlands and forests, over the bleakest moorlands of the Pennine Hills, or the dense thickets and gushing streams that peppered the lower grounds, merely served to confirm the king's unenviable reputation of being unpredictable. Abruptly halting his riding-party mid journey to attend a feast at a remote lodging house, he would leave his stranded host kicking their heels in frustration. Similarly, at the break of each new dawn, he would despatch hurried instructions to the rested camp to suddenly uproot and move onwards without even the slightest hint of a warning. During his leisure periods, Henry would hunt, hawk, play chess, feast, discuss affairs of state or enjoy witty conversation, but also frequently indulged in intimate liaisons with a string of women which was perhaps the most pleasurable of his pursuits. His queen, Eleanor of Aquitaine, was in her thirties at the time of their marriage, and their relationship produced five sons and three daughters. As the years grew by, the ever-virile Henry fathered at least a dozen illegitimate children, including four by Alice de France, daughter of Louis VII, and at the time, fiancée of his own son, Richard. Henry's vigorous sexual appetite knew no bounds and was well known to all at court. The Bishop of Oxford once remarked, 'He [Henry] was at no period of his life a faithful husband, and when he had quarrelled with Eleanor, he sank into sad depths of licentiousness.' As regards the matter of Henry's personal hygiene, he was not so enthusiastic and during the period of his reign, England had not yet subscribed itself to the bath culture that was prevalent in the Mediterranean and elsewhere, and the records of official payments given to royal bath attendants indicate that the king took a bath, on average, once every three weeks, giving rise to the impression of an unwashed king awash with gold. Henry's father, Geoffrey, had hailed from Anjou, a region of mediaeval France situated to the south of Normandy, and during his lifetime, Geoffrey became the ruling count of Anjou. The royal house of Anjou became better known to history as the Plantagenets, from the words *Planta Genista*, being the Latin name for the broom, a sprig of which was habitually worn by Count Geoffrey on his helmet. According to ancient legend, an ancestor of the Plantagenets was a witch named Melusine who one day flew out of the window of her earthly castle never to return. Bitter opponents of the family would often openly sneer – 'From the Devil they came, to the Devil they will go.' Others maintained that the Angevins revealed their 'devilish' ancestry during the fiendishness of their temper.

From the moment that Henry reached his temporary quarters, which are believed to have been Chester Castle, the chief residence and headquarters of every ruling earl of Chester since the Norman Conquest, he would have been the recipient of the finest hospitality that his eminent position so demanded. Guests of honour at a mediaeval banquet would be treated to a spectacular evening of feasting, and those assembled inside the Great Hall woud have been pleasantly overcome by the delicious aroma of a myriad of prepared dishes. Sprinkled with an assortment of herbs and spices, examples of extravagant offerings of the period included peacock, boar, goose and chicken. A typical feast could also include goat, veal, stag, pigeon and eggs. Some seven or more centuries earlier, cheese had formed the staple diet of the Roman legions of Chester, and they had taught the Cheshire farmers the secret of its manufacture. Delicious cheeses made from the milk of the local deer herds, shaped in a mould, also featured on the typical menu of important gatherings. The Dee's finest salmon, freshly plucked from the bubbling rapids of the Cheater Weir, sodden and baked with verjuice, would be regularly consumed, so too a selection of local marine edibles, including mackerel and oysters, cockles and mussels, and eels in crust. For those whose appetite was still not pacified, there would be an ample supply of simnel cakes ready to devour. With hunger satisfactorily conquered, man's natural thirst would also need to be addressed. During this period, beer was the most common drink throughout England, but wine was deemed to be of greater prestige, the white version even more so than the red. Although there were numerous vineyards scattered throughout England, their final product was considered inferior to the imports, therefore the taste buds of the nobility were far more accustomed to the foreign flavour. From the depths of the naturally cooled cellars, an endless supply of wine would be hurriedly despatched to the dining chambers above, and there poured into tall goblets that never seemed to drain. Whilst in Chester, Henry was attended by Malcolm IV of Scotland, there to perform homage. In 1153, Ranulph II, earl of Chester, died, leaving his son, Hugh, still only a minor, unable to actively engage the position of his inheritance. Nevertheless, the earldom's developed bureaucracy continued with seamless efficiency, as a justice, two chamberlains, the constable of the castle, the clerk, and the earl's reeve and sheriff maintained law and order.

During the course of his long reign, Henry II enjoyed an endless cycle of hospitality wherever he went. During the normal routine of his daily existence as England's head of state, the king's royal household consisted of an incredible 270 members, the majority of whom were permanently attached to the court. The officials of Henry's court can be roughly divided into five groups of diminishing importance. The first group included his chancellor, the stewards, the master-butler, the master-chamberlains, the treasurer and the constable. The second group included the three master-dispensers, the master of the writing office and the deputy of the master-chamberlain. The third group was made up of the deputy constables and the master-marshal. The fourth group included the deputy dispensers, and the fifth the minor officials such as the porter of the king's bed, and the ministers to the king's sport. Among the ranks of the royal service, there included a fruiterer, a master-cook of the king's kitchen, a bearer of the alms dish, a dispenser of the larder and the master-dispenser of the household bread and wine. Further roles included keepers of the cups (four would serve together in turn), four horn-blowers (paid three pence daily), and wolf-catchers of the king's forest (paid twenty pence daily). For his chancellor, Thomas à Beckett, who fulfilled a vital role during Henry's reign as the first subject of his kingdom and was said to have accompanied the king everywhere, his daily income was said to be five shillings, one royal simnel cake, two of dripping, an offering of clear wine, an offering of household wine, and one wax candle and forty candle ends. Historical sources relating to the Welsh campaign of 1157 do not actually reveal the exact number of Henry's household that accompanied him to Chester, but it has been suggested that a large contingent routinely followed the king during his regular movements throughout the realm.

From this point of the campaign, the Welsh chronicles fortunately provide us with a documented general outline of the course of Henry's expedition into north-east Wales and the inevitable Welsh response. Leading the way are four Welsh chronicles which almost certainly derive from a single written source, the substance of each of them, however, has been independently

Chester Castle
Built by William I in 1070, this was the chief residence and headquarters of every Norman earl of Chester.

abbreviated to varying degrees from the common original. Three of the chronicles are in Welsh, namely *Brut y Tywysogyon* (The Chronicle of the Princes, Red Book of Hergest version), *Brut y Tywysogyon* (The Chronicle of the Princes, Peniarth Ms 20 version), *Brenhinedd y Saeson* (The Kings of the Saxons), and *Annales Cambriae* written in Latin.

According to these chronicles, at the start of the 1157 campaign, Henry established his army's maiden camp at a station called 'the marsh of Chester' or 'the open land of Chester' and there 'he [Henry] pitched his tents.' In the Welsh language, this area was known as Morfa Caer Lleon, meaning 'the marsh of the fort of the legions', and later it became better known to all as 'Saltney Marsh', an extensive tract of marshland that enveloped the southern shore of the Dee estuary, from the area below Chester Castle to the sands of Wepre (an area now part of the modern day town of Connah's Quay on Deeside, Flintshire). This seven-mile stretch of dreary and largely uninhabited sea-land, once described as 'two thousand acres of legion defying swamp', formed an ideal location to accommodate a large military camp containing thousands of soldiers. Subjected to flooding at every tide, the terrain of this local marsh was cursed by the powerful onrush of gushing waters; the labyrinth of gullies, gutters and ditches filling to capacity to deny a safe passage to any human traffic. It seems logical that Henry's army, aware of this dangerous natural occurrence, would have safely pitched their tents on the reliable pieces of dry land adjacent to the marsh.

The gloomy estuarine landscape that invited and accommodated oblivion was newly transformed into a vibrant tented city crammed to capacity with men drawn from every corner of England. Much is known of Henry's methods of raising soldiers for campaigns, and narrative accounts attest to his ability to summon the hosts of England, and if needed Normandy and Anjou, with relatively little notice. There were foresters and millers, butchers and quarry men, labourers and cloth-makers in camp, every one of their number being an able-bodied man between the age of fifteen and sixty. Many of them brought into camp the trusted tools of their daily professions, freshly sharpened axes and long handled scythes and common knives, soon to be wielded in the fight against the men defending northern Wales. Those better endowed possessed broad-headed spears, quartered helmets of iron and gambesons (a padded protective jacket). The majority of the levy wore no armour, neither did they bear recognised figures, colours, shapes and designs on shields, banners and tabards (a sleeveless jacket consisting only of front and back pieces with a hole for the head). Although the Bayeux Tapestry (a length of fabric depicting scenes from the battle of Hastings) shows commanders carrying banners, while some of the shields depicted bear both abstract and figural images, it is believed that during this particular period of mediaeval history, armorial bearings were extremely rare and exclusive to only a very small number of the Anglo-Norman aristocracy. The earliest examples of heraldic arms among the Anglo-Norman baronage are the 'checky' (chequerboard) design of Count Waleran of Meulan, earl of Worcester (d 1166) and the chevrons worn by Gilbert de Clare, earl of Hertford (d 1152). A company of Shropshire archers, marshalled by William

Saltney Marsh today. During the mediaeval period, a great salt marsh stretched from Chester to the modern-day Connah's Quay.

FitzAlan, the wealthy sheriff of that county and a dedicated adherent of Henry II, trundled into camp. Some of them wore white hats to shade their eyes from the sun during battle and their impressive six feet long bows, manufactured mainly from the yew, were slung across their backs. The trained archers of the age were bracketed as the *corps d'elite* of the battlefield, a highly skilled and greatly feared force of mostly foot-soldiers who could expectedly overcome the dual challenge of mounted knight and infantryman alike. With startling velocity, in one single minute an experienced archer could loose a dozen arrows with total accuracy at a target of up to 200 yards away. Archers carried several kinds of arrows with different heads, some long and pointed intended to pierce mail as if it were linen; others broad and curved intended to inflict crippling flesh wounds on their target. The shaft was manufactured from ash and the end embedded with plucked goose feathers and averaged twenty inches in length, and the bowstring would be made from hemp or a similar fibrous material.

War is a dangerous business, and in order to maintain the wellbeing of an army in the field, the availability of medical supplies was a crucial necessity. Mediaeval armies on campaign would carry rudimentary first aid kits with soft linen bandages to treat the wounded, an assortment of natural or herbal medicines to anaesthetise the seriously maimed prior to operations, and wine and urine as useful antiseptics. Operations carried out on the campaign trail could easily end in death as post-operative infections were extremely common. It must also be acknowledged that the din of noise generated in a mediaeval camp was horrendous, as was the stomach-churning stench generated by the odious bodily odours that emanated from a travelling community whose membership ran into thousands. Baggage of every description would be slung across the drooping backs of horses, or piled high upon cumbrous

A twelfth-century Anglo-Norman knight, showing the typical straight-legged riding style.

two-wheeled wagons made of rough planks; some suffering the incon-
venience of derailment on the rough roads leading into camp as their owners
frantically executed necessary repairs. Of course, with such a gargantuan
enterprise there appeared the bands of greed-ridden opportunists. Akin to a
plague of parasites, local traders based in the nearby towns would fervently
flock into camp, seeking to serve this vast assembly of men with plentiful
offerings of corn, fresh meat, and wooden casks filled to capacity with beer
and wine, all at a price. For the wealthy Anglo-Norman nobleman on campaign
and the ordinary English soldier in camp, the drama, discord and drudgery
of a war in an alien environment had started in earnest.

8

The huge well of resources available to Henry from his English kingdom never ran dry and in 1157 the wealthiest, best-governed state in Europe prepared to unleash its ferocity upon the northern Welsh kingdom of Gwynedd. In the wake of Henry's royal council held at Northampton on 17 July 1157, it was inevitable that the news of Henry's intent would stretch into the Gwynedd court.

Owain Gwynedd duly summoned his own forces in a defiant call to arms. Our knowledge of Welsh military strategy in the mediaeval period suggests that some form of an organised armed resistance was already in motion on the eve of Henry's staged arrival in Chester. Let us imagine that, from the precise moment that the forces of invasion began to assemble upon the marshes of Chester, a contingent of Welsh spies would have successfully pinpointed the position of the royal army and maintained an ever vigilant eye upon the Anglo-Norman camp. To the immediate west of the Chester marsh stand a chain of hills that dominate the skyline forming an ideal vantage point for the benefit of peering eyes. But, during this critical stage of the campaign where exactly was Owain Gwynedd and his army? Could the vastly experienced, but greatly outnumbered Welsh leader mount a credible challenge to such a large deployment of troops stationed on the threshold of his kingdom?

During the twelfth and thirteenth centuries, Gwynedd was recognised as the most powerful of the native Welsh kingdoms. Geographically blessed by a largely impregnable landscape, the heartland of the ruler's power lay in a region called Gwynedd Uwch Conwy, the lands to the west of the river Conwy, naturally shielded by the imposing mountain ranges of Snowdonia. On the eve of Henry II's campaign of 1157, Owain Gwynedd also held Gwynedd Is Conwy, the region to the east of the river Conwy known also as Perfeddwlad (the Middle Country) or the Four Cantrefs. In its full extent, therefore, the kingdom of Gwynedd consisted of a broad arc of territory in north Wales, extending from the river Dee to the river Dyfi which defined the border with the region of Ceredigion in western Wales. Moreover, occupying the entire north-west area of Wales, Gwynedd confronted the Anglo-Norman territory around Chester to the east, the land of the rival Welsh kingdom of Powys to the south-east, and the Welsh kingdom of Deheubarth to the south. The kingdom was suitably protected against hostile incursions from any of these directions by an expanse of imposing mountain barriers, including the uplands of the Clwydian Range, Cadair Idris, Hiraethog and Migneint, and of course the Snowdon massif. Gwynedd was further blessed by having the luxury of fertile lands, including the grain growing territories of Anglesey and the Llŷn Peninsula. In particular, the island of Anglesey, known variously as Mona (Latin), Anglesey (Norse) and Ynys Môn (Welsh), was romantically viewed as the traditional source of food for the whole of Wales.

The kingdom of Gwynedd was home to a civilised society, and the people adhered to an established system of laws. The traditional Welsh laws were named after Welsh king Hywel Dda (died c 950) and were remarkably liberal for their time, focusing on restitution for specific crimes committed within the community rather than

A thirteenth-century illustration of a
Welsh spearman poised to strike.

violent punishments. For example, the crime of murder was punished by way of a compensation payment towards the family of the deceased, instead of the perpetrator being put to death. Furthermore, a person caught stealing food might be pardoned if he could prove that he had been begging in vain for three days in an attempt to feed his starving family. These codified laws served almost every occasion, including the legal status of women in Welsh society. It is clear, therefore, that the kingdom of Gwynedd was socially developed, self-supporting, and politically organised.

During the mediaeval period, Wales was divided into several autonomous regions called *gwladoedd*, the largest of these being Gwynedd, Powys and Deheubarth. Each *gwlad* was divided into districts called *cantrefi* or hundreds, meaning one hundred settlements (or towns) and each *cantref* was divided into two or three *cwmwdau* (commotes). For example, as part of Owain's kingdom of Gwynedd, the *cantref* of Llŷn was divided into the *cwmwdau* of Cymydmaen, Dinllaen and Cafflogion. The leader of the *gwlad* could either be called king, prince or lord (*brenin, tywysog* or *arglwydd*) and it was the leader's family who enjoyed the highest status in the kingdom. As the ruler of Gwynedd, Owain was supported by an administrative body of court officials whose duty was to serve, counsel and escort their sovereign when and wherever needed. In addition, Owain was also dutifully served by an established household guard, a *comitatus* — in Welsh a *teulu*. This important body of men was more than simply an armed household guard, it was an elite fighting force of mounted soldiers who, from the twelfth century onwards, was as well trained and suitably equipped as its Anglo-Norman counterparts. Historians estimate that the twelfth century rulers of Wales had at their command a serving *teulu* of around 120 to 140 men, a figure which could swell during periods of war. In comparison, the more powerful Anglo-Norman barons were able to command a *comitatus* or personal bodyguard of around 30 to 40 men. Among the body of royal officers attached to Owain's court, there included the *penteulu* (captain of the household guard), the *distain* (steward), the *bardd teulu* (poet of the war band), a priest, judge, falconer, huntsman and chief groom (master of horse). In each commote, Owain had an established lesser court house which served as the focal point of local government, where the *rhaglaw* (local officers) held their court. From time to time, Owain, in the company of his entire court, embarked on a royal progress around the commotes of his kingdom. During these routine visitations, local appeals were heard, the ruler's dues were received and the work of his local officials was reviewed. During periods of warfare the Welsh rulers relied upon their personal *teulu* and all freemen of fighting age to form the army (sometimes referred to as '*llu*' or 'host'). When a Welsh leader summoned his subjects for war, only those individuals who were classed as freemen in Welsh society were eligible to bear arms. When the leader levied his army the 'unfree' could tag along to perform menial tasks such as ditch digging and transportation duties, but they were strictly prohibited from fighting. According to the ancient laws of Wales, military service was a privilege and the length of an individual's military service was dictated by circumstances. If the homeland was invaded by an enemy force, the length of service was unlimited, but service outside of the *gwlad* was restricted to no more than forty days, thereby allowing men the option to return home if desired. The Welsh freeman warrior was a hardy specimen, brave and uncompromising, and was trained to live off the land and endure considerable hardship. Furthermore, the best of the warriors could be selected to join the leader's elite war band and would therefore be entitled to ride into battle on horseback. Within the free class were two levels, the *uchelwyr* (nobles) and the *boneddigion* (freemen), the latter being the sons of the former. In essence, the head of a Welsh family was classed as a noble and when he died his sons became nobles and received a share of their father's lands. Below the free people were the *taeogion* (bonds people), followed by slaves and foreigners who lived in Wales.

During the mediaeval period, the typical Welsh soldier was viewed by his

A thirteenth-century illustration of a Welsh archer.

enemies as a robust and brutal killing machine. Trained during the period of his youth to master the skills needed to kill opponents, every youth in Wales was purposely fed an endless theme of war stories, glorifying the bloodied deeds of past encounters. This ingrained culture reliably delivered a conveyor belt of fresh warriors eager to serve their overlord and master. A Welsh soldier on campaign was expected to move nimbly across difficult terrain, endure episodes of extreme hardship and adverse weather conditions, and instinctively strike an enemy with every means at his disposal. Contemporary accounts of the fighting prowess of Welsh soldiers are numerous, the vivid description written by the religious chronicler, Gerald of Wales, forms a prime example:

> They [the Welsh] are passionately devoted to their freedom and to the defence of their country: for these they fight, for these they suffer hardship, for these they will take up weapons and willingly sacrifice their lives ... It is a remarkable fact that on many occasions they have not hesitated to fight without any protection against men clad in iron, unarmed against those bearing weapons, on foot against mounted cavalry. They are so agile and fierce that they often win battles fought against such odds ... The English fight for power; the Welsh for liberty; the one to procure gain; the other to avoid loss. The English hirelings for money, the Welsh patriots for their country ... if they would become inseparable, they would be insuperable ... they deem it a disgrace to die in their bed, an honour to die in the field of battle.

An Anglo-Norman chronicler described in graphic detail a typical clash with a Welsh force:

... one of our soldiers, in a battle against the Welsh, was struck by a Welsh arrow in the thigh. It penetrated through his padded cloth hauberk and right through his leg armour, and this same arrow then passed on through his saddle flap and deep into his horse, mortally wounding it. Another soldier was likewise hit by an arrow and into his saddle. When he reigned his horse round in a half circle, moreover, a second arrow shot by the same archer hit him in the other thigh, so that he was firmly fixed to his horse on both sides ...

Even kings of England acknowledged the fighting properties of the Welsh race. Henry II would later write to Manuel Comnenus (d 1180), emperor of Constantinople, informing him:

In a certain part of the island [of Britain] there is a race of people called Welsh, so bold and ferocious that, when unarmed they do not fear an encounter with an armed force, being ready to shed their blood in defence of their country, and to sacrifice their lives for renown ... the Welsh are a wild people who cannot be tamed.

Henry's son, Richard the Lionheart (d 1199), would later write of the fighting men of Wales whom he took with him on the Third Crusade:

For though they may be routed today, ... tomorrow they are ready for another campaign, quite undaunted by their losses ... they are deterred neither by hunger or cold, fighting does not exhaust them, nor adversity cause them to despair: after an overthrow they immediately rise again, ready to face the hazards of warfare once more ...

Describing the marked differences between the armies of Wales and their opponents from England, a contemporary Welsh account records:

There they [the Normans] fight on plains, here in rough terrain;
they fight in fields, we in woods;
their armour is honourable, here it is a nuisance;

they win by standing firm, we by agility;

they capture the enemy, we cut off his head;

they ransom prisoners, we slaughter them.

Confronted on his border by such a mighty force headed by England's finest knights and militias, the ruler of Gwynedd did not betray the natural instinct of his race. By moving his outnumbered ranks towards the vicinity of Henry's tented army, an unprecedented manoeuvre for a Welsh ruler, the calculating Owain not only daringly answered Henry's challenge to battle, he actually chose the precise location for the campaign's opening encounter.

During the build-up to war, it was the responsibility of the ruler's local officer or bailiff, the *rhaglaw*, to organise the gathering of men and materials, usually at the location of the recognised commotal centre, and in the summer of 1157, the able-bodied men of Gwynedd dutifully answered Owain's call to arms. In the cantrefs of Arfon, Arllechwedd, and Llŷn, the warriors gathered, as did their comrades in Ardudwy, Meirionnydd, Eifionydd and Môn. Surviving evidence supporting the actual size of Owain's army in 1157 is non-existent. However, based on recorded figures attributed to other Welsh forces of the mediaeval period, a calculated estimate is certainly achievable. During the autumn of 1136, an alliance of native Welsh rulers, including Owain Gwynedd, was said to have raised a force of 8,100 men (6,000 infantry and 2,100 cavalry) for a campaign in west Wales. In the winter of 1282, Llywelyn ap Gruffudd (Llywelyn the Last), with allies, embarked on an ill-fated campaign in central Wales with 7,160 soldiers (7,000 foot soldiers and 160 horsemen). Evidence suggests that in 1157, Owain Gwynedd stood markedly alone, his fellow Welsh rulers proving indifferent to his cause, or even more damaging, a group of them joining King Henry as allies. Therefore, a figure of somewhere between 2,000 and 3,000 soldiers forming Owain's army is certainly a plausible calculation.

Every Welsh infantryman wore a belted, linen shirt, simple linen shorts or breeches, and a *brychan*, a long woollen blanket used for daily wear, battle, and ultimately, burial. In battle, the Welsh infantrymen would use a range of weaponry including scythes, agricultural axes, billhooks, simple slings and rough looking bows. Those better equipped engaged their opponents using long knives, spears and wooden shields, and those even more favourably blessed had their heads crowned by a simple iron helmet.

To reach the war zone, the soldiers of Gwynedd crossed heather moorlands, extensive woodlands, rolling green hills and river valleys, but never once during this laborious trek would they have suffered the pain of thirst or famine. Thanks to predatory hunting skills, a nutritious bounty of rabbits, hares, birds and fish would be scooped and snared from the Welsh countryside. The soldiers would also have consumed on the campaign trail the meat of cattle, pigs and sheep, together with cabbages, beans and wild berries. Although food was plentiful, this could in fact create problems. The history books are filled of reports of armies consuming uncooked food, and as a consequence, suffering outbreaks of dysentery. Likewise, local water supplies could seldom be relied upon; ideally wine or mead was drunk by all if infections were to be avoided.

Of the soldiers who formed the ranks of Owain Gwynedd's army, the most impressively dressed on campaign were those who belonged to the body of the *teulu*. This elite fighting force of loyal soldiers consisted of the kingdom's best warriors and the important office of *penteulu*, the chief of the royal retinue, was held by a prestigious person, usually one of the ruler's sons. When journeying towards the theatre of war, the *teulu* would always be mounted on horses. The royal court of Gwynedd enjoyed an impressive stud of horses, and according to the Welsh laws, the king would be served by a personal escort of 36 persons on horseback. Furthermore, every chief officer of the royal household had a horse permanently supplied by the king. A particular favourite of the Welsh soldiery was the cob, a short-legged, but powerfully built, barrel-chested horse. Owain Gwynedd, and a handful of his *teulu*, would also have possessed a foreign horse, or destrier, a specialised war horse of high quality, most probably acquired either by purchase or theft. It is likely that the majority of Owain's *teulu* attired themselves for a battle in stolen equipment. The Welsh found plunder a less expensive if not more convenient means of acquiring the latest military hardware. As is generally recognised, the cost of equipping a man from head to foot for war was quite considerable. Add to this the cost of obtaining and maintaining a warhorse and it becomes clear that the business of war was beyond the means of all but the very rich. Good quality horses were extremely valuable. Under Henry II a standard price appears to have been £2, though one was bought for £6 13s 4d (£6.67). Even before a mediaeval battle was over, the stripping of the dead was a routine habit . On account of this, during a battle the majority of the *teulu* would be similarly dressed to those wealthy Anglo-Norman nobles on campaign: sleeveless tabards, a long shirt of mail, a padded jacket, mail leggings, leather riding boots and a mail coif worn beneath a helmet. Furthermore, the teulu carried into battle a lethal combination of weaponry, including long-shafted spears, axes and swords, and maces and daggers. In addition, the use of a flat-topped, kite-shaped shield protected the upper part of the body and tapered downwards to protect the left leg.

On the eve of the 1157 hostilities, Owain Gwynedd stationed his forces at Basingwerk, a fact recorded in all four versions of the Welsh chronicles. Basingwerk has a long history. In or around 1131, monks from the abbey of Savigny in south-west Normandy established a monastic community at Basingwerk in north-east Wales, and in 1147 the monasteries belonging to the order of Savigny were incorporated within the Cistercian order, including Basingwerk. The original chapel was known both as the chapel of Basingwerk and the chapel of Coleshill. Previously, the site had been known as Dinas Basi and it later became the site of a motte and bailey castle, commonly known in the modern day as 'Hen Blas'. In essence, the weight of evidence strongly suggests that the historic names of Dinas Basi (Dinas Basing), Coleshill

Chapel, Basingwerk Chapel and Hen Blas all relate to the same place. Immediately after Henry's campaign of 1157, the monks at Basingwerk moved to new premises at nearby Fulbrook (Greenfield), taking the recognised name with them, a manoeuvre that has confused some historians into erroneously believing that the surviving Basingwerk Abbey at Greenfield was where Owain Gwynedd located his camp in 1157.

The original Basingwerk is in fact located one-and-a-half miles to the west of the modern day town of Flint and is part of the parish of Coleshill Fawr in the Flintshire village of Bagillt. The site is strategically blessed and is perched on the brow of an eminence at the confluence of two streams which have scoured out ravines to a depth of more than fifty feet at their junction. In addition, occupying a projection of land that stands almost 300 feet above sea level, the post is ideally placed for guarding the narrow coastal strip between two prominent watercourses, the Lead Brook (situated in modern day Oakenholt, Flint) and the Fulbrook (the Holywell Stream). Located above the estuary of the Dee, the site also presents a perfect vantage point for the monitoring of passing ships. The evidence indicates that the area of Basingwerk was taken by Owain Gwynedd during the period 1146–50. In 1150, he recorded an impressive battlefield triumph at 'Coleshill', and by crushing the combined forces of Ranulph II, earl of Chester (d 1153) and Madog ap Mareduud, ruler of Powys, cemented his grip on the important border territory of Tegeingl.

During the summer of 1157, the place called Basingwerk was transformed into a military zone, the picturesque landscape of rolling green pastures, gushing streams and leafy groves sloping gently to the shores of the Dee, surrendering to the customary pre-battle activities. Akin to a colony of industrious ants, the Welsh soldiers in camp must have worked admirably in preparing their defensive positions to counteract the threatened full-frontal assault from Henry's oncoming war machine. Any theories that suggest the process of mediaeval warfare lacked strategy or military intelligence and

Hen Blas, Bagillt, Flintshire
Various versions of the Welsh chronicles testify that in 1157 Owain Gwynedd took up his
forward fortified position at a place called 'Basingwerk'. The weight of evidence leads
modern historians to believe that the original Basingwerk is likely to have been situated at
Hen Blas in Bagillt, overlooking the river Dee.

tactics are fuelled by ignorance and prejudice. In relation to the Welsh field preparations for the summer war of 1157, the content of the Welsh chronicles clearly confirm a meditated approach to battle : '... against him [King Henry II] came Owain Gwynedd and his host, as far as Basingwerk. And there a site for a castle was measured and huge dykes raised' (*Brenhinedd y Saeson — the Kings of the Saxons*, text and translation by T. Jones, 1971); and '... then, after Owain, prince of Gwynedd, had summoned to him his sons and his forces and his might, he encamped at Basingwerk, and a mighty host along with him. And there he made an appointment for battle with the king and had ditches raised with the intention of giving open battle to the king' (*Brut y Tywysogyon — the Chronicle of the Princes*. Red Book of Hergest Version, text and translation by T. Jones, 1955). The 'huge dykes' and 'ditches' raised at the scene of Owain's camp at Basingwerk were presumably a measure to hinder and disrupt any assault upon the Welsh lines, a tactic not uncommon for the period and sometimes markedly successful. Before the impressive Scottish victory at the Battle of Bannockburn in 1314, the Scottish leader Robert the Bruce selected a defensive position before instructing his men to dig a series of small pits covered with brushwood to protect his flanks. And, at the Battle of Crecy, 1346 , in northern France, a series of small pits and ditches were constructed by the English forces in order to derail the powerful and greatly feared French cavalry, where at least fifteen cavalry charges failed to break the English front line, resulting in a remarkable English triumph.

The tract of marshland occupied by Henry's tented army is shadowed by the first high ground to the west of Chester on the route to the uplands of Tegeingl (modern day Flintshire), the vale of Clwyd and the castle of Rhuddlan, and the commanding ridge incorporates the landmark of Hawarden Castle, its ruins still visible today. Whether or not this prominent hill was cloaked in woodland in 1157, and contemporary accounts lead us to believe that it was, it afforded an excellent sanctuary for inquisitive eyes locked on the Dee marshes below. This ridge, incorporating today's Bilberry Wood and

Looking towards the wooded ridge of Bilberry Wood/ Warren Mountain from the ancient road between today's Broughton and Hawarden. Routes from the east had to pass this dominating feature.

Warren Mountain, has for some been a tempting spot to imagine as the place where Owain Gwynedd's scouts saw for the first time the sheer magnitude of the Anglo-Norman army. As the impending clash of arms drew closer, Owain Gwynedd and his 'leading men' finalised their own strategy for battle.

But, who in fact were these 'leading men' that formed Owain's trusted circle of royal officers? Sadly, their names are not generally known. Every one of Owain's able-bodied sons of fighting age took part in the campaign of 1157, including Dafydd (d 1203) and Cynan (d 1174), two dependable warriors who were importantly tasked by their father to spearhead the first Welsh assault of the campaign. Certain sources indicate that the important role of distain (steward) to Owain was occupied by Hwfa ap Cynddelw (d c1169), an Anglesey nobleman whose estate was believed to be centred around Presaddfed. It was said that the role of distain was his office by inheritance, giving him the right to bear the ruler's coronet on state occasions. Another prominent nobleman of Anglesey who was said to have served Owain as a hereditary dignitary was Llywarch ap Brân, a figure listed by some sources to be Owain's brother-in-law. Another presumed member of Owain's retinue was a man named Aser. Among others who served Owain was the renowned warrior-poet Gwalchmai ap Meilyr (d c1180), a man who saw active service in Owain's *teulu* and who, when delivering one of his poetic compositions, had proudly sung to the royal court,

> Gwalchmai am I called, a foe to the English.
> Bloody is my sword and fierce in battle
> In the tumult of the host I am a killer
> Multitudes praise me that have not seen me.

Dutifully served by a crowd of loyal followers, Owain also enjoyed the intimate support of the Welsh church. Some clerics fulfilled the role of diplomatic messengers, men like Moses and Guirdas, who delivered Owain's letters to the French king, Louis VII, in Paris. Owain once described Guirdas as 'my private and familiar cleric'.

Although Owain ruled the kingdom of Gwynedd, he never once styled himself as the king or prince of Gwynedd. As early as 1140 he styled himself as *rex Walliae* or king of Wales, and from around 1166 onwards embraced the title of prince, using either *Waliarum Princeps* (Prince of Wales) or *Walensium Princeps* (Prince of the Welsh) in official letters. Even in England, Owain's elevated status appeared to gain recognition. In three letters written between May and September 1169, Archbishop Thomas à Becket addressed Owain as 'prince of the Welsh'.

In the manner of soldiers throughout history, the army of Gwynedd would have whiled away the hours in camp by hunting and resting, the rank and file blessed by a rich abundance of natural resources. The air in a mediaeval camp was dominated by a myriad of smells, the delicious scent of cooked animal fats, choking fumes generated by burning wood and the pungent waft of horse excrement. Bundles of wood gathered from the surrounding forests fuelled the camp fires and trees harbouring a luxury of fruits and thick hedgerows dripping with berries provided the picker with vital sources of nourishment. Delighting man's appetite further, the small mammals habitually prowling the forest floor were eagerly hunted. Welsh soldiers resting on campaign would have entertained themselves with idle chatter and communal laughter and played traditional piped music. Of course, as the black mass of evening descended, the men in camp would have tried to settle down to sleep, despite the following dawn promising the furious advent of battle.

9

Emerging from the gates of Chester Castle in the summer of 1157, King Henry II led a powerful procession of knights. We can speculate that the weather conditions on that particular summer's day must have been favourable to Henry's cause as the respective chronicles of England and Wales fail to mention the occurrence of adverse elements such as a heat wave, drought, gale or heavy rain. Henry's impressive cavalcade of men would have crossed the river into Handbridge and set out on the designated route into northern Wales.

Henry's plans would have been carefully laid. By choosing Chester as an initial base for military operations, he had the use of an established and vibrant port. In addition, the city was surrounded by a protective chain of motte and bailey castles, strategically constructed along the English border to deter Welsh raids — the fortresses at Shotwick, Aldford, Pulford, Dodleston and Hawarden were routinely occupied by small garrisons. Henry tactically deployed a two-pronged thrust against Owain Gwynedd's prepared entrenchments at Basingwerk, and by dividing his army into two distinct divisions, believed an ensnarement of the Welsh positions would be the key to success on the battlefield. The king's land army was supported by a large naval force on the seaward side, providing him with unrivalled supremacy at sea against the Welsh defenders.

According to the chronicles, the king's land forces followed the route of two common roads into north-east Wales. One division, boasting 'many earls and barons beyond number, and with them a strong force fully equipped'

(*Bruty Tywysogyon,* Peniarth MS20), negotiated a course consistent with the shoreline of the Dee estuary; and the other, described by the same Welsh chronicle as 'an innumerable armed host, fearless and ready for battle', advanced under Henry's personal leadership along the stretch of densely wooded hills that run parallel to the Dee estuary between Hawarden and Basingwerk.

When Henry and his 'innumerable armed host' entered the Tegeingl forest, the king firmly believed that he commanded the local heights. But, unbeknown to him, a band of Welsh fighters lurked among the dense avenues of trees and unruly thickets. Marching intently along a tree-strewn ridgeway peppered with an array of small rolling hills, steep-sided ravines, sodden valleys and rushing streams in narrow cuttings, Henry's unsuspecting division of men included some of England's premier knights. The king's personal troop included the figure of Eustace FitzJohn (d 1157), a powerful magnate of northern England and a celebrated veteran of numerous campaigns. During a colourful career, he had founded the abbey of Alnwick in Northumberland and the abbeys of Watton and Malton in Yorkshire, and was endowed with the office of Constable of Chester. Also with the king was Henry de Essex, a regular of the royal court, who held the office of Royal Constable. Previously, he had served as the sheriff of Bedfordshire (1155),

Old Dee Bridge, Chester. The original wooden bridge was replaced by a stone bridge in the late thirteenth century

and by hereditary right was bestowed the prestigious honour of being the king's standard bearer. Roger de Clare, earl of Hertford (d 1173), nicknamed 'the Good Earl', and Robert de Courcy (d 1157), a proud veteran of many military expeditions and a baron of great distinction, also accompanied Henry's strong division of men.

The king's warhorse would have worn a mail bard over its body, as did those mounts ridden by the wealthiest of the barons, whilst others wore fitted head and chest defences. The barons were customarily served by two attendant squires — one in front carrying the baron's wooden-shafted lance, one behind, leading the spare horse or horses (during the Battle of Hastings in 1066, it was said that Duke William of Normandy had three warhorses killed beneath him). At the onset of battle, typically signified by a medley of horns, the lance-bearer handed his knightly master the lance and then charged after him on the spare warhorse.

During twelfth-century warfare there were surprisingly few distinctions of rank in a mediaeval army. The term sergeant could indicate a multiplicity of things, from an ordinary infantryman to a mounted sergeant, armed and horsed in much the same way as a knight. Commanders in the army could be referred to as 'constable' or 'marshal'. Predominantly, the knights, squires and sergeants formed the core of royal armies (the sergeant's inferior status to the knights was later demonstrated by the rabbit-fur trimming on their robes, while knights had squirrel fur). Although the actual size of Henry's force in 1157 remains impossible to ascertain, an examination of other royal campaigns provides several examples of the numbers that were recruited into the king's army. During King Edward I's war against Llywelyn ap Gruffydd, ruler of Gwynedd, in 1276/77, the English king probably maintained 15,500 paid footsoldiers when the army was at its largest. The greatest number recruited for service in Wales was believed to have been during the countrywide revolt of Madog ap Llywelyn in 1294/5 when at one stage of the campaign there were possibly over 36,000 soldiers enlisted in

By choosing Chester as his base for military operations against Owain Gwynedd, Henry's position was adequately protected by an established network of motte and bailey castles at Aldford (left), Dodleston (middle right), Pulford (middle left) and Shotwick (bottom).

the various English armies. Wales was renowned as a hazardous country for any invading army, full of major geographical obstacles such as meandering rivers, mist-shrouded mountain ranges and heavily-cloaked forests, forming a terrain that had the potential to derail even the most deep rooted of strategies. As a consequence, there existed in England a much stronger tradition of military service in the border regions than in other parts of the country, the conditions of a frontier society creating a greater militarised environment than elsewhere. According to the Domesday Book, the burgesses (free citizens) of Shrewsbury and the tenants of Hereford had to accompany the sheriff on expeditions into Wales. In addition, the men of Archenfield in Herefordshire customarily provided the vanguard (the leading part) of armies entering Wales and the rearguard (the soldiers positioned at the rear) on their return. Further evidence suggests that the county of Cheshire probably saw a higher percentage of men recruited into the royal armies of mediaeval England than any other county in the kingdom.

It is easy to form the argument that Henry II should have comfortably won any war against Owain Gwynedd, given the great mismatch of resources between the two armies. However, a campaign commander wishing to maximise the clear advantages in his possession would need to display outstanding organisational skills to deliver outright success. During a century or so of sporadic warfare between the Anglo-Norman invaders and the defending Welsh rulers, battle honours were evenly balanced. Both had enjoyed notable victories and both had suffered resounding defeats, but neither had secured an overwhelming supremacy in Wales. Although the fearsome Norman war machine had not yet achieved the conquest of Wales that was comparable with their defining success in England, the increasing number of established Anglo-Norman lordships throughout Wales proved the marked presence of an alien virus intent on multiplication. From the time of the Norman Conquest of England in 1066 to the beginning of Henry's reign in 1154, the ruling kings of England had launched five royal expeditions into the interior of Wales. Incredibly, during the first eleven years of his reign, Henry II would match this figure by personally leading five expeditions into Wales: 1157 (northern Wales), 1158 and 1163 (southern Wales), and twice in 1165 (northern Wales). Of the numerous invasions of Wales undertaken by the kings of England during the 1066–1415 period, not one reigning king of England had met his death whilst on campaign there. During the summer of 1157, Henry II was to come tantalisingly close to suffering such a fate.

The swirling morning mist that moves mischievous across the lively estuary waters forms an eerie grey mass that spills across the Dee shoreline and beyond. A mile or so inland, the king of England and his juggernaut army lumbered westwards. During the Roman occupation of Britain an infantry-man on campaign would have been expected to cover a distance of twenty miles in five hours. But by the mediaeval period, armies on campaign had become much more cumbersome, weighted down as they were with weapons and vital provisions. Nevertheless, a march from Chester to Basingwerk (Coleshill) could still have been accomplished in one day. Between the opposing campsites there existed a substantial forest and, according to contemporary accounts, the sprawling kingdom of greenery almost choked the entire surface area of the *cantref* of Tegeingl. The Domesday Book of 1086 had described the *vills* of Wepre and Golftyn (both part of modern-day Connah's Quay), Leadbrook (part of modern-day Flint), Aston, Hawarden, Broughton, Fulbrook (modern-day Greenfield) and Halkyn as possessing varying amounts of woodland. The *vill* of Hawarden was described as being 'two leagues long and one league wide' (approximately six miles by three miles). Two hundred years later, during King Edward I's invasion of Tegeingl in 1277, the coastal plain was so heavily wooded that a large body of labourers and woodsmen were required to clear an extensive area of the forest, so as to ensure the invading army a much easier and safer passage through a quiet and sparsely populated district. It is quite likely that shortly after entering the leafy dome of this vast forest, Henry's marching army disappeared from view.

In the shadow of the present-day ruins of Hawarden Castle runs an old route into north-east Wales. Still visible today, the sunken way —often mistakenly called 'the moat'— was possibly in use many centuries before the Romans came and it probably served the invaders of 1157. The castle at Mold had fallen to Owain Gwynedd in 1146, but there is no evidence to support the theory that this reversal of Anglo-Norman power in the region was mirrored at Hawarden, indicating that in 1157 the castle there was still in the hands of the Anglo-Normans. Avoiding the route that ran along the shore of the Dee, which was habitually riddled by the menace of gurgling quicksands and dark salt pools, the king's army would have advanced through the woodland, the vanguard leading the way forward. Careful not to venture too far from the perceived safety of the trodden pathway, their tentative probing was essential to the army's well being. The able-bodied vanguard included scouts, cavalry and light troops followed by the main body of heavy infantry. The fore-riders of the vanguard would be accompanied by the harbingers, whose job was to locate lodgings for the army. The theory that mediaeval armies marching through relatively unknown territory would haphazardly stumble their way through the countryside is flawed. On almost every occasion, the route chosen by an army was based upon local knowledge. Using pre-existing road systems or trackways, a number of which had been forged by the Roman engineers, armies would follow a tried and trusted route. Many of these lay alongside rivers or streams and were regularly travelled by local inhabitants, drovers and pilgrims.

Concealed by clouds of rising dust, the King's army tramped along the wooded ridge that connects the woods of Hawarden and Wepre, crossing three prominent streams — the water courses known today as the brooks of Broughton, Wepre and New Inn. These streams, that are today still heavily cloaked by woodland, would have been crossed by means of fords located at their narrowest points and, as Henry's soldiers crossed, the white splashes of water would have risen as high as the saddles of the riders, the horses

The 'Sunken Way', Old Hawarden Castle, Flintshire. Below the ruins of the castle runs the course of the old main road from Chester to Conwy, which is often mistaken for a moat.

quivering and shaking their manes as they waded across the cold streams.

The large body of knights that formed the king's household troop surrounded the sovereign, strong, elegant, majestic and menacing. Their armour gleaming in the summer sun as they rode boot to boot, the hooves of their magnificent horses tossing small clods of disturbed earth behind them. The need to identify a knight of high status, whose face and head was concealed by his helmet, nose guard and mail coif, was especially acute during the confusion of a mediaeval battle and a small number would have worn distinctive colours adorning banners, shields and tabards. The tradition of warriors bearing symbols and emblems into battle was ancient. The Roman legions had followed their eagles and the Bayeux Tapestry shows commanders carrying banners, while some of the shields depicted bear both abstract and figural images that would have been easily identifiable. Martial symbols and emblems were thus not new, although the elaborate, rule-governed heraldry did not emerge until the closing years of the twelfth century.

For the majority of the conscripted soldiers, the prospect of spending up to six weeks away from home could easily derail enthusiasm for the task ahead. In fact, the greatest enemy that confronted all mediaeval armies apart from fighting, famine and sickness, was the curse of desertion. The Anglo-Norman armies suffered a constant haemorrhaging of men, and desertion from the ranks would begin the moment levies left their county muster points. These were not professional soldiers and they had left homes and domestic duties behind them, which must, for all the hardships of the time, have appeared preferable to the squalor and drudgery of life in camp. Even in the moments leading to battle, men, frozen by fear, would openly run from the battlefield to preserve their lives. During the recruitment phase, abuses were rife, local officers were offered bribes so that the military service might be avoided.

Trueman's Hill Motte, located close to the centre of the village of Hawarden. Some believe this to be the original site of Hawarden Castle. A popular local tradition maintains that this was raised in 1157 as a fortification to prevent Henry II from advancing by this route into Wales.

Old Hawarden Castle, the focal point of the Anglo-Norman lordship of Hawarden.

Despite having the advantage of the high ground, Henry and his column would soon come to a shuddering and untimely halt. Detached from their comrades entrenched at Basingwerk some seven or so miles away, a band of Welsh fighters lay concealed in the cavities of the Tegeingl forest, giving the impression that almost every copse and dell and defile was infested by the armed warriors of Gwynedd. Strong, agile and fit, their bodies fuelled by adrenalin, the detachment of men commanded by Dafydd and Cynan prepared to unleash their unbridled fury on Henry's ranks.

The deliverance of a memorable victory, however, could not be assured as every one of the oncoming Anglo-Norman horsemen, weighted down in their saddles in their mail attire, represented the equivalent of a human tank. Furthermore, detailed archaelogical examinations of skeletons from this period revealed that Anglo-Norman cavalrymen possessed large neck muscles and although their legs were regarded as small in length, their muscles were also large. As the designs of helmets resulted in them becoming heavier, neck muscles grew, and the leg muscles of such soldiers were always strongly developed as a consequence of riding such powerful warhorses. In

Wales, during the mediaeval period, it is easy to understand how opponents so dangerously and strongly equipped swept the landscape, leaving behind them a bloody trail of swords, skulls and strongholds.

As Henry's marching division drew closer, the concealed ranks of Welsh soldiery viewed their foes in silence. Crouching amidst the undergrowth, not daring to move a muscle, their lithe frames were poised to strike. And then the enemy appeared, the ground shaking with the thunderous vibrations created by a multitude of marching feet and hooves. Suddenly, one lengthy blast delivered from a Welshman's horn would pierce the air, and the Welsh fighters proceeded to unleash a ferocious attack upon the stunned and haplessly exposed Anglo-Norman soldiers.

The opening of any mediaeval battle would have been extremely noisy. Fuelled by a combination of anger, fear, adrenalin and aggression, men would scream, yell, curse and rage at one another. Summoned to battle by a spine-tingling medley of horns, the Welsh soldiers would charge through the thickets, creating as much noise as possible in an attempt to destroy the enemy's morale. When the woodland battle began, there was no doubt a great sense of confusion. Armies in England during the mediaeval period usually followed a clearly deliniated battle pattern from its opening to conclusion. Initially, long-distance weaponry, namely archery, was unleashed to maim, kill and terrify the enemy. Secondly, a full-blooded cavalry charge was employed, followed by the general engagement, the melée, and finally, the rout when an enemy would be absolutely destroyed and all those who remained standing would be mercilessly pursued from the scene of the battlefield and slaughtered. In the woodlands of Tegeingl, this pattern of fighting was impossible to employ. Although the Welsh were regarded as able soldiers, their style suited that of the guerrilla fighter, and their favoured method of engagement was never better demonstrated than during Henry II's first encroachment into Wales.

As screaming bands of Welsh infantrymen launched a blizzard of rocks and other projectiles at the serried ranks of Henry's army, a body of their archers loosed a deadly volley of arrows into the Anglo-Norman soldiery. With cold-hearted precision, they drew and loosed, reloaded, then drew and loosed again, repeating the formula relentlessly as the fearsome storm of white feathered, metal-tipped shafts hissed and whistled through the air. It was not uncommon for archers to deliberately dip the tips of their arrows into excrement, human or otherwise, thus creating an early form of biological warfare. An arrow was able to travel further and faster than anything else on the battlefield and was capable of taking a man off his feet. A skilled archer could rightly boast that he held twelve lives on his girdle, and it was said that in one minute alone, his six-foot bow could discharge a dozen arrows with devastating effect.

As the two forces collided with a thunderous crack of iron and wood, mailed horsemen, with only their eyes visible, screamed in fear when being pulled from their tall warhorses by the nimble actions of the Welsh daggermen, who venomously plunged their gelid steel blades into the vulnerable undercarriages of the terrified beasts. Some riders toppled sideways from their neighing mounts, rivers of blood spilling down their faces as they hurtled towards the ground that was newly lubricated with entrails and discarded armour. The riders' wooden lances, an average of fourteen feet in length, were of little use in such a consolidated melée. Likewise the wooden shields, if penetrated by a spear, forced the owner to discard his first line of defence, thus offering himself as an open target. A chorus of sickening thuds perforated the air as Henry's exposed divisions were systematically cut to pieces, the axes smashing limbs and ribs and even the heads of the horses.

The area of the battle formed a terrifying crucible of head-clasping horror. Swords, brilliant devices for slicing and hacking through bone, found soft obliging tissue and the sharpened, silvery-grey metal was forcibly thrust into the interior of the body. The sounds of hundreds of swords being unsheathed resonated as soldiers were decapitated or tumbled to the floor minus a hand,

Hawarden Woods, the scene of an ambush of Henry's forces, quoted in Brut y Tywysogyon.

an arm or a leg. As men fell wounded, choking and gurgling in their own blood, fear gripped a score of the combatants, who decidedly turned their bodies away from the carnage and, without striking a further blow, hurriedly fled the field.

Locked into the mechanics of dozens of brutal scrimmages, the throng of bulbous-eyed combatants grimaced, snarled and winced as they proceeded to clobber, club and batter one another into oblivion, their ferocious encounters creating a cacophony of noise. It was butchery on a grand scale, blessed by royalty. Each soldier fought grimly and desperately, reliant on his own resources. Men discarded their weapons, lost teeth, jewellery, clothes and links of mail. Suffocation was another battlefield curse, perhaps feared above all others. As men violently collided, the sheer press of their bodies could crush the air from their lungs. Fighting on a warm day led to additional dangers, in particular the life-threatening symptoms of dehydration and heat exhaustion. Such wilful destruction of human life knew no bounds and the

Broughton Brook. Rivers are often thought of as the reliable roads of the forest. In 1157, an army marching along the wooded ridgeway connecting the manors of Hawarden and Wepre would have been forced to negotiate three prominent watercourses – the brooks of Broughton (above), Wepre (right) and New Inn (left).

examination of mediaeval skeletons has proved just how sickening it was to be embroiled in such ferocious encounters. A preserved skeleton from the Battle of Sterling Bridge in Scotland (1297) had more than one hundred fractures, thirty of which were on the skull. The injuries sustained were often the equivalent to those suffered by a modern-day victim of a high-impact car crash. Moreover, in a forest or rough ground, which customarily breaks up organised formations, a large, armoured division is forced into a distinct disadvantage. Less aware of what is going on around them, they are far slower to react to a prepared enemy bearing down on them. Panic quickly sets in and groups collapse and run. In the woodlands of Tegeingl in 1157 this is precisely what occurred. The Welsh fighters forced Henry's advancing division to fight on a narrow front, thus greatly minimising the effect of their numerical advantage. King Henry, reacting to the grave danger that threatened to overwhelm him, admirably thundered into action. Potentially, he was only one blow away from death. Sitting rigid in the saddle, his head straight and heart pounding, he braced himself to enter the perilous zone occupied by the mass of writhing bodies locked in combat. The surviving chronicles are silent regarding the king's actual conduct during the heat of this battle, but they testify that the king was rumoured to have been killed during the early stages of the attack and that a distinctive cry on the battlefield informed all within earshot that Henry had been slain. As the shocking word of the king's death quickly spread through the ranks of the Anglo-Norman force, their fears must have intensified, creating widespread panic and uncertainty. There was nothing better suited to the Welsh manner of fighting than a mass retreat by a large force. Withdrawal could easily be turned into a rout, a measured withdrawal harried into headlong flight and order broken into disorder. In the king's personal retinue, Eustace FitzJohn and Robert de Courcy both lay dead.

At some stage during the course of the woodland battle Henry successfully removed himself from the centre of the killing zone, 'And after many of the

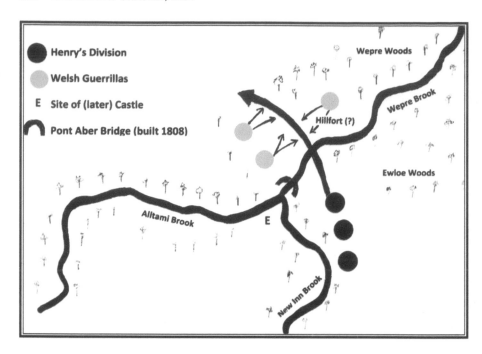

'Battle of Ewloe, 1157'
This battle map is based on the tradition of placing the ambush of King Henry's forces in the vicinity of the woods of Wepre/Ewloe, near to the confluence of two ravines occupied by two streams. This tradition has been popularised by numerous bodies, including local history societies, and a plaque commemorating the Battle of Ewloe was unveiled at Pont Aber/Wepre Park Bridge in 2008. However, according to J. Veninger in her thesis 'Archaeological landscapes of conflict in twelfth-century Gwynedd' (University of Exeter, 2015), placing the ambush here is a misidentification of the site and a section of her thesis claims that the terrain in this area, dominated as it is by steep ravines, narrow ridges and cliff outcrops, is unsuitable for the execution of a succesful 'guerilla' operation.

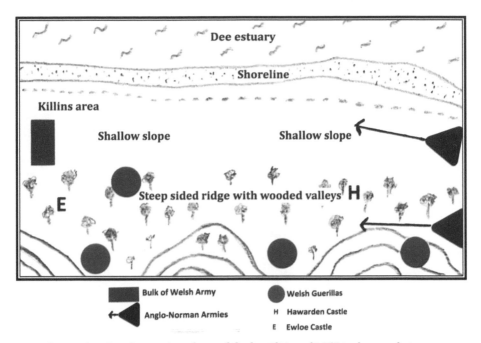

A map showing the opening phase of the hostilities of 1157 in the area between Hawarden and Ewloe, based on M. Hackett's interpretation of events (Lost Battlefields of Wales, 2014).

A campaign map of 1157, based on J. Goronwy Edwards' interpretation of events ('Henry II and the fight at Coleshill: some further reflections', Welsh History Review, v 3, 1–4, 1966–7). The author's understanding of events places the approximate site of the fighting between Ewloe and Hawarden.

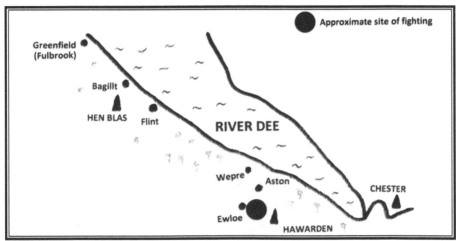

Mediaeval re-enactment societies Cwmwd Iâl, House of the Black Star and Les Miles des Marches, recreate a twelfth-century woodland battle between the forces of Henry II and Owain Gwynedd.

king's men had been slain, it was with difficulty that he escaped back to the plain' (*Brut y Tywysogyon, the Red Book of Hergest*). Astride his powerful warhorse, his mailed fists tightly clenched, Henry reportedly undertook a brave and desperate gallop to safety. Riding through an avalanche of arrows, spears, and missiles to reach a place of relative safety, his life was miraculously preserved and his reputation still intact.

The same, however, could not be said of others. The man justly held responsible for wrongly declaring the king's death on the battlefield was Henry, earl of Essex, the king's personal standard bearer. His conduct during this historic encounter has echoed down the centuries and many writers have cast him in the role of a coward. His mistaken declaration of the king's death at the height of the woodland ambush would certainly have created hysteria among Henry's fighting ranks, and perhaps caused soldiers rushing from the rear, desperate to assist the battered vanguard, to turn on their heels and join the growing exodus of retreating soldiery. For a man of Essex's pedigree to faithlessly cast down the royal standard and flee for his life, he must have encountered a degree of butchery in the woodland that was on a terrifying scale, even for such an experienced soldier. As the prized royal standard fell to the forest floor, so too did the earl's reputation. According to the *Chronicles of Jocelin of Brakelond* (1173–1202), Roger, the earl of Clare (d 1173), charged to the scene with his personal entourage and successfully raised the banner of the king for the fleeing ranks to see, an act which 'revived the strength and courage of the whole army'. Jocelin, we are told, obtained his information first-hand from Henry de Essex himself.

The action of Roger, earl of Clare, transformed a seemingly irreversible situation into one of renewed hope, undoubtedly preventing an even greater loss of Anglo-Norman life. Whilst escaping the murder and mayhem in the forest, those combatants who fled formed a pitiful sight, the mighty royal army reduced to a pathetic blood-stained rabble. As the scattered units of soldiery stumbled from the wood into the open meadows overlooking the

Dee, a commander of lesser mettle witnessing such miserable scenes may have turned his face away from the challenge, choosing retreat over redemption. Henry II, however, did not betray his steely resolve and commendably regrouped his shattered force.

There is a lack of evidence relating to what occurred after the ambush. The only extant evidence suggests that Henry continued to push westwards along the wooded ridgeway of Tegeingl, but makes no reference to any time scale. Did Henry's fragmented force continue its advance towards Basingwerk some seven miles away, or did the battle-weary force initially establish a camp in the vicinity of the ambush?

Despite the terrible losses inflicted upon Henry's army in the ambush, the king had not lost the war and, even more crucial to the potential success of the Anglo-Norman enterprise, the power of Owain Gwynedd's calculated assault had failed to stem the tide of invasion. After slaying what must have amounted to hundreds of enemy soldiers, the victorious soldiery of Gwynedd vacated the woodland graveyard. On foot, mountain pony and warhorse, their torn clothing stained berry-red by blood, the booty-laden force, led by Dafydd and Cynan, withdrew westwards towards the direction of the Welsh camp at Basingwerk.

It must be appreciated that mediaeval battles had no set pattern of action and their duration is often something of an enigma. The Battle of Tinchebray in France (1106) was probably concluded in one violent hour, and Agincourt (1415) lasted no more than two or three hours. In contrast, the Battle of Morlaix in France (1342) was halted on three occasions, so tired and out of breath were the combatants and Bannockburn (1314) was said to have lasted for two days. One source theorises that the Battle of Hyddgen in Wales (1401) was possibly divided into three phases spanning several days. In the case of Henry's campaign of 1157, no sources exist to reveal the actual timespan of the woodland battle; or even the duration of the campaign itself.

Being intercepted at the midway point of his measured advance from

The arms of King Henry II. The two golden lions on a crimson field had been the arms of Normandy. In 1152, Henry II married Eleanor of Aquitaine whose emblem was a single lion on a crimson field. After Henry's death, the lions were joined together to form the now familiar three lions used by the monarchs of England.

Chester to Basingwerk, Henry was forced into an armed combat much earlier than he had anticipated and the scale of the engagement and the significant casualties suffered could possibly have delayed his move towards the Welsh entrenchments, which were still half-a-day's march away from the scene of the ambush. There are grounds for assuming that some of the fighting had occurred somewhere close to the site of the castle of Hawarden. A contemporary poem, penned by Cynddelw Brydydd Mawr (d. *c.*1200) the chief court poet of Madog ap Maredudd's Powysian court, states that Bleddyn Fardd, a young warrior poet attached to the same Powysian court, died in the battle 'below the court of Pennardd', which must refer to Pennardd-alaog,

Hawarden Castle Park

Elegy for Bleddyn Fardd of Powys (d 1157)
sung by Cynddelw Brydydd Mawr

In battle-tumult the scattering of a host, in the thick of battle a battle-host
Defending before the most valiant one;
Under blades dealing out death,
Under a blue shield a hero has been slain.
There has been slain a youth of flawless verse (it is no fault to honour him)
Below the court of Pennardd,
A terror in battle, of irresistable courage,
One who loved the van, one of wolf's fury was Bleddyn Fardd.
An exalted and magnanimous poet, a poet nurtured long on mead
And lengthy pratice of horsemanship,
His whole intent was to attack,
His renown brought him his wealth.
When his battle-fury wrought a path for his fame,
O! warriors of England who beheld him,
O! nobles of Powys, which was the swifter:
A flame, or the wolf-leap of Bleddyn?
Bleddyn, a wolf in the breach, met his death with honour,
He slew a greater number (of his enemies),
A young man of mead-nurtured upbringing,
A boy in years and the grief for him the greater (because of that).
Most deeply does the deep pain of his taking away pierce me,
A cruel one in claiming his right in a fierce attack
Wherever red blood flowed,
A torrent upon a spear at the ready.
The sword of the one who was ardent in versecraft was ready
On the day of battle by Chester strand,
One swift to anger, a shield in a hundred battles,
A hero, a splendid hero, a foremost slayer in battle.

now Penarlag, the Welsh name for Hawarden. The 'court of Pennardd' would presumably be the castle of Hawarden. Furthermore, Cynddelw Brydydd Mawr's elegy for Bleddyn Fardd states that 'On the day of battle by Chester strand (*traeth Caer*)', a strong suggestion that the fighting spread from the forest of Hawarden on to the area of open ground facing Chester across the Dee.

Dafydd and Cynan had played their part to perfection in the murderous encounter, but the ambush did not end the conflict, but instead served only to fuel an evolving battle of wills between the two equally determined commanders.*

* The battle maps devised by M. Hackett and J. Goronwy Edwards are certainly plausible considerations. However, piecing together an account of the campaign, the preparations for it, the action itself and what happened afterwards, is extraordinarily difficult. Likewise, if we consider with a degree of caution that Owain Gwynedd had under his command some 2,500 fighting men, it is not wholly fanciful to envisage the deployment of such numbers as listed below.

> 500 men stationed on the island of Anglesey, commanded by Hywel ab Owain Gwynedd.
> 1,000 men occupying entrenchments at Basingwerk/Coleshill, commanded by Owain Gwynedd.
> 500 men in the western sector of Hawarden Wood (the present day Ewloe Wood), commanded by Cynan ab Owain Gwynedd.
> 500 men in close proximity to Hawarden Castle/Court, commanded by Dafydd ab Owain Gwynedd.

10

The blood spilled during the brutal encounter of 1157 made an indelible imprint across the pages of the mediaeval chronicles and the memory of the woodland encounter has endured the ages and continues to attract the attention of modern day historians. Based on historical sources, the battle is known variously as the Battle of Hawarden Wood, the Battle of Ewloe or the Battle of Coleshill. But, where in fact did the fighting of 1157 take place?

Based on the evidence of the surviving chronicles, the sanguinary engagement between Henry's division and the force commanded by Dafydd and Cynan took place in a wood, but, confusingly, two alternative locations for this have at various times been suggested. One is based upon the writings of Geraldus Cambrensis (Gerald of Wales) and partly upon the chronicle of Jocelin of Brakelond and the *Annals of Chester*. The latter do not in fact mention the wood, but both locate the fighting in 'Coleshill'. Jocelin says that the hostile action occurred 'in the difficult pass of Coleshill', while the Chester annalist records that the battle took place *'apud Colsul'* [next to or at Coleshill]. Gerald's writings are more detailed, describing how in 1188, during the course of his journey around Wales with Archbishop Baldwin of Canterbury, he slept the evening at the priory of Basingwerk (not to be confused with the original Basingwerk foundation in Coleshill), and he writes as follows:

The following day we traversed a long quicksand, and not without some degree
of apprehension, leaving the woody district of Coleshulle, or hill of coal, on our

right-hand, where Henry II, who in our time, actuated by youthful and indiscreet ardour, made a hostile irruption into Wales, and presuming to pass through that narrow and woody defile, experienced a signal defeat, and a very heavy loss of men.

Beginning with David Powell in 1584, a succession of writers have taken Gerald's phrases, *'silva de Koleshulle'* and *'silvestria de Coleshulle'* to mean a wood belonging to, and therefore situated within the bounds of, the *vill* of Coleshill. Coleshill is recorded in the Domesday Survey of 1086 as the name of a *vill* (town). The boundaries of that *vill* were perpetuated in the later township of Coleshill, which occupied an area of some three square miles, immediately to the west and north-west of the later borough of Flint. This view was eventually enshrined in the six-inch Ordnance Survey map which marked the fields adjacent to Coleshill Farm (in the area of Coleshill Fechan) as 'Supposed site of the Battle of Coleshill (fought in 1157)'.

Evidently, a score of modern day historians have similarly subscribed to the view that the fighting occurred somewhere inside the *vill* of Coleshill, most notably D. J. Cathart King, the author of 'Henry II and the fight at Coleshill' (*Welsh History Review*, v2, 4 (1965), pages 367–73). Therefore, the quoted references to 'Coleshill' as being the place where the ambush and fighting of 1157 took place have traditionally been assumed to represent the *vill* of Coleshill. However, Coleshill also became the name of quite a sizeable recognised commote, extending in length some eleven miles, approximately from Whitford to Wepre, and in breadth some three miles, up-country from the Tegeingl (Englefield) shoreline of the Dee estuary, possibly established following the conquest of the region by Owain Gwynedd in the 1140s. There is at any rate the marked coincidence that Henry II, after his summer campaign of 1157, fortified three castles in Tegeingl (Englefield) — Basingwerk, Prestatyn and Rhuddlan — and that Tegeingl was organised into three commotes, called respectively the commotes of Coleshill, Prestatyn and

Ewloe, Flintshire. According to M. Hackett in Lost Battlefields of Wales, *this sloping ridge, from the area of Ewloe Castle to Killins Lane (located in the present-day Higher Shotton), is where Owain Gwynedd deployed the bulk of his army prior to the commencement of a 'running battle'.*

Rhuddlan, which may well indicate that the three commotes of Tegeingl had already been formed by 1157. It was a recognised action of the Anglo-Normans who attempted to conquer Wales in the eleventh and twelfth centuries, to treat the Welsh commotes as their 'units of penetration', by setting up in each commote a castle to serve as its military and administrative centre. Fundamentally, Gerald's statement that the fighting took place in 'the wood of Coleshill' is rendered ambiguous by the consideration that Coleshill may have referred either to the *vill* or to the commote of that name.

The two alternative sites that have been proposed for the battle royal of 1157 are therefore the wood of Coleshill, and the wood of Hawarden. The mystery behind Gerald's references to Coleshill, however, does not affect the pivotal point which is established by the best-informed evidence available that the location of the 'hard battle' was in the wood called 'the wood of Hawarden'. Modern day historians have acknowledged the fact that the contemporary Welsh chronicles are very detailed about the campaign of 1157, regarding their content as by far the best informed source of information that is available. Based on the evidence of the Peniarth MS 20 version of *Brut y Tywysogyon*, the conclusion seems inescapable that the scene of the ambush and attack upon Henry's division was somewhere within the confines of Hawarden Wood: a passage clearly states,

> And the king and an innumerable armed host, fearless and ready for battle, came through the wood which was between them, which was called the wood of Hawarden. And there Cynan and Dafydd, sons of Owain, encountered him, and there they gave him a hard battle.

In acknowledgement of this crucial source of information, a number of prominent modern historians have nominated Hawarden Wood as the scene of the fighting, including Sir J. E. Lloyd and Sir J. Goronwy Edwards.

But, where exactly inside the woods of Hawarden did the fighting occur? As mentioned above, the Domesday Survey of 1086 records that the manor of Hawarden possessed an area of woodland measuring 'two leagues long and one league wide'. which indicates that Hawarden had a greater area of woodland than any of its immediate neighbouring *vills* (Wepre, Broughton, Aston and Golftyn). Traditionally, the native inhabitants of Hawarden practised their farming in cleared areas of the extensive forest. However, from the seventh century onwards, Anglo-Saxons from Mercia and Cheshire moved in to displace the indigenous Welsh, and their evolving influence spread to neighbouring areas and a series of *tuns* [settlements or farmsteads] were established at nearby Aston, Bretton and Broughton. During this period of transition, it seems likely that a wooden fortification was constructed at Hawarden. Penarddalaog (sometimes Pennardlaawc) was the name of a wide area, familiar to the native Welsh. The period of alien domination, however, gave the settlement itself a new name — Haordine [Hawarden]. Consequently, the Welsh communities were forced to re-settle in areas to the west and south of the town and continued to use the woodlands for their livelihood. T. W.

'Fools Field', Ewloe. According to local oral tradition, Henry II camped here prior to (or after) being ambushed by Dafydd and Cynan, the sons of Owain Gwynedd.

Pritchard, in his *A History of the Old Parish of Hawarden* (2002), proposes that the 'predominantly Welsh communities west and south of the town continued to use Pennardlaawc of lands and woods further west (Koet Pennardlaoc — Hawarden Wood) and they continued to call the town Penardlaawc (Kastell Penardlaoc — Hawarden Castle).' The theory of such a distinction, between the established settlement on the eminence and the woodlands to the immediate south and west, offers an insight into tracing the location of the Koet Pennardlaoc (Hawarden Wood) of 1157 as mentioned by the *Brut y Tywysogyon* MS 20. Given the fact that the recognised Welsh manor of Ewloe and the English lordship of Hawarden later became neighbours, there is a possibility that the area recorded as 'Ewlawe' in the 1280s formed a part of the 'Koet Pennardlaoc' of 1157.

In 1584, David Powel published a tome entitled *Historie of Cambria (Brut y Tywysogyon — the Chronicle of the Princes* is more or less a straight record of events, whereas the *Historie of Cambria* elaborates on and extends the original). This was the first monograph to be published on the history of

Wales and it soon became a primary reference for generations of historians. Intriguingly, the fact that David Powel substitutes 'Coed Eulo' for the previous 'Koet Pennardlaoc' may indicate a more precise location for the initial clash. However, it must be stressed that David Powel does not indicate his reference or evidence for 'Coed Eulo' (Ewloe Wood) and his interpretation must be treated with extreme caution. Evidently, a small number of modern historians have followed Powel's lead by placing the Welsh ambush of Henry II somewhere inside Ewloe Wood. For example, an essay, written by Edward Parry for the Royal Denbigh Eisteddfod in 1828, titled 'The Flintshire Castles', for which the author obtained the Society's medal, includes the following passage:

> Adjoining the castle of Ewloe, there is a wood, still called Ewloe Wood, very celebrated for the memorable repulse that a part of the flower of Henry the Second's army received in 1157 from David and Conan, sons of Owen Gwynedd.

Following on from this account, William Henry Gladstone (1840–91), the former Liberal Member of Parliament for Chester and High Sheriff of Flintshire, records in *The Hawarden Visitors' Hand-Book*, revised edition, 1890:

> About one mile and a half from Hawarden on the road to Northop, lie ensconced in a wood the scant remains of the Old Castle of Ewloe — the scene of a battle between the English and Welsh in 1157, in which the former were defeated by David and Conan, sons of Owen Gwynedd.

An article in the 1957 *Publications of the Flintshire Historical Society*, v 17, 'Notes on Excursions: Soughton Hall, Northop Church, Ewloe Castle' by George Lloyd, mirrors the same theme:

Against this invasion of Henry, the two sons of Owen, Dafydd and Cynan, took up an advanced position in the woods at Ewloe, probably in the vicinity of the present ruined castle. Here Henry's advance guard was completely ambushed and thoroughly defeated.

Moving on to more modern accounts of the battle, T. W. Pritchard also links the vicinity of Ewloe Castle with the assault on Henry: '

Just below Ewloe Castle (to the north), is the confluence of the Alltami Brook and the New Inn Brook (to form the Wepre Brook). In 1157 Henry II was ambushed here in 'Koet Pennardlaoc', 'the wood of Penarlag'.

Vic Williams, author of *The Great Estate (The Early Years), Wepre Hall* (2004, pp 19–20), and a leading authority on the history of the ancient manor of Wepre, locates the ambush as being '... in the woods at Wepre and Ewloe' and '... in the narrow defile of Wepre Woods ...'

Clearly, these accounts all locate the ambush to the vicinity of Ewloe Castle, situated on a narrow ridge approximately 100 metres above sea level, the remains of which are still surrounded by extensive woodland. It is thought that this woodland represents all that remains of the once great mediaeval forest of Tegeingl, described by the eighteenth-century writer Thomas Pennant as '... deep and darksome, forming a most gloomy solitude' (*Tours in Wales*, 1774, v 1, p88).

Nothing actually exists in the form of primary sources to link the area of Ewloe Castle with the Welsh ambush on Henry's division. However, a strong local oral tradition continues to flourish, and a commemorative plaque was placed here in 2008 along with a small exhibition inside the nearby Wepre Park Visitor Centre. Interestingly, a stone footbridge, spanning the Wepre brook, erected in 1808, was originally called Pont Saeson (The Bridge of the English). Unfortunately, why this bridge was so-named remains a mystery.

The bridge originally stood half a mile or so away at the head of the Wepre Valley but was removed to its present location in 1808 and renamed Pont Aber. It must be stated that the native Welsh stronghold of Ewloe Castle was probably built sometime after the events of 1157. This area of Wepre Park / Ewloe Wood is in fact steeped in history: the Wepre Brook (river) is believed to have once formed the ancient boundary between Wales and the Saxon kingdom of Mercia, and it has been suggested that, before that period, a tribal hillfort existed on the heights overlooking the river's traditional crossing point. The site is marked on the Ordnance Survey as 'Fort' and is known locally as Bryn Gaer. This has, for some, been a tempting spot to imagine as the site of the battle and only a small leap of imagination is required to envisage a force of Welsh fighters commanded by Dafydd and Cynan perched on the summit of Bryn Gaer prior to their charge down the hill to engage an unsuspecting enemy. The wooded area beneath Bryn Gaer appears untouched by the modern age, a statement backed by the guide book *Discover Wepre Park*.

> Wepre's woodlands are ancient and untouched by man. Wepre's woodland floor has never been cultivated or built on, and its meadows and ponds have never been improved or drained.

In contrast, recent opponents of the Ewloe Wood theory have proposed that although the terrain favours concealment, it is not ideally suited for the execution of a fleet-footed ambush and speedy withdrawal, two crucial components of what we might now term 'guerrilla' warfare.

11

Returning to the actual campaign , the force of Welsh soldiers led by Dafydd and Cynan hastily vacated the woodland, leaving behind the carnage inflicted by them on the king's force. Henry II is believed to have had a phenomenally foul temper and this military setback must have adversely affected his mood. A number of historians have labelled Henry's calculated manoeuvre into the woodlands of Tegeingl as a reckless and naïve act. The king's tactics, however, were faultless; his detachment was powerful, it was well-led and included many seasoned campaigners of high calibre, and despite the best efforts of the Welsh, his force had survived the setback to recommence the strategic two-pronged thrust against the Welsh entrenchments at Basingwerk. Evidently, Henry's armoured division resumed their westward march along the wooded heights of Tegeingl, the men, horses and provisions negotiating the rough, unpaved trackway shielded by trees and ridges. And, as they did, each and every member of Henry's blood-stained force must have focussed on the surrounding greenery, strongly suspecting a follow-up assault from the same Welsh fighters who had drawn first blood.

Meanwhile, inside the precincts of the Welsh camp at Coleshill, some six or so miles away from the bloody arena of the woodland battleground, Owain Gwynedd would have been anxiously awaiting news of the outcome of the campaign's first armed encounter. It is conceivable that the Welsh ruler was totally oblivious to the fate of his two warrior sons and the dangerous operation that he had tasked them to perform, which could easily have resulted in their deaths. Owain had already lost his youngest son, Rhun in

1146 and was therefore not a stranger to personal grief. When news of the success of his sons eventually reached him, he found himself faced with a new dilemma — should he remain at his fortified station at Coleshill in anticipation of a full-blown assault against his lines, or should he abandon the camp

Pont Aber, Wepre Woods, Connah's Quay. Originally called Pont Saeson (English Bridge) it was demolished at its original position further up the Wepre valley and rebuilt at its present site.

and remove his forces to a more favourable location? The chronicles inform us that Owain chose the latter option. *Brut y Tywysogyon — the Red Book of Hergest* records:

> And when Owain heard that the king was coming against him from the rear side, and he saw the knights approaching from the other side, and with them a mighty host under arms, he left that place and retreated ....

However, in defiance of this evidence, David Powel, wrote in 1584 that Henry 'was in great danger of his life in a strait at Counsylth (Coleshill) not far from Flynt' and that there was an earlier engagement at 'the wood called Coed Eulo', but makes no mention of a source for these statements. Other writers have subsequently embraced Powel's words. Henry Taylor in *Historic Notices of Flint* (1883) wrote, 'After inflicting great loss upon the English at Ewloe, the Welsh were ultimately repulsed at the Battle of Coleshill' and T. A. Glenn, in *Excavations at Llys Edwin, Celyn Farm, Northop* (1934) stated,

> The first engagement is said to have been in the woods of Euloe where the advance guard of the English force was ambushed and driven back. Henry,

Bryn Gaer, Wepre Woods, Connah's Quay, Flintshire. Directly overlooking the traditional crossing point of Wepre brook.

Below: Wepre Woods, Connah's Quay, Flintshire. Standing guard alongside the course of the Wepre brook is this stone sculpture of a mediaeval soldier, a clear reference to the locality's links to mediaeval history.

Below: Wepre Woods, Connah's Quay, Flintshire. According to V. Williams in his book The Great Estate (The Early Years), Wepre Hall, Connah's Quay, *2004, 'Henry personally led a contingent of troops up through the valley of the Wepre brook while his main force marched along the river bank.' According to a local tradition, this prominent copse, in the lower half of the Wepre valley, is where some of the fighting of 1157 took place.*

however, avoiding that pass, again moved forward in the direction of Northop, entering, finally, a wooded valley leading to the hamlet of the *vill* of Coleshill, where he was attacked on all sides in great force...According to local tradition, the battle took place in the pass or meadow between Llys Edwin and Bryn Edwin, on the border of the *vill* of Coleshill, a field yet known as 'battle'.

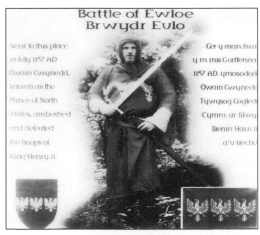

The commemorative plaque in Wepre Park, Connah's Quay, which was unveiled in 2008, by Carl Sargeant, the serving Assembly Member for Alyn and Deeside.

In fact, the author muddies the waters even further when affixing this 'second' battle to a location standing more than two miles away in distance from the *vill* of Coleshill, namely the pass between Llys Edwin (in Northop) and Bryn Edwin (in Flint Mountain).

Any attempt to reconstruct the events of Owain Gwynedd's measured withdrawal from his camp at Basingwerk (Coleshill) would be an exercise laden with difficulty. Nevertheless, despite the absence of contemporary evidence, and given that all the surviving manuscripts clearly reference only one armed engagement, there still endures a powerful local tradition that a second clash occurred somewhere within the confines of the *vill* of Coleshill. The historic village of Bagillt incorporates the townships of Coleshill Fawr, Coleshill Fechan, Bagillt Fawr and Bagillt Fechan and forms the breeding ground of this tradition. This belief is further strengthened when studying the six-inch O.S. map which marks the fields adjacent to today's Coleshill Farm (in Coleshill Fechan) as 'Supposed site of the Battle of Coleshill (fought in 1157)'. Furthermore, *The Royal Commission on Ancient and Historical*

Llys Edwin, Northop, Flintshire. T. A. Glenn (Excavations at Llys Edwin, 1934) records that Henry II may have made his headquarters at the historic site known today as Llys Edwin and 'destroyed it on leaving.' It must be noted that Glenn's source that gives rise to this statement remains unknown.

Monuments and Constructions, An inventory of the Ancient Monuments in Wales (1911) states,

> The spot marked on the Ordnance Map as the supposed site of the battle of Coleshill (1157), though any one, or all, of the adjoining fields in the township of Coleshill Fechan would suit the required conditions.

Interestingly, an area of Bagillt village called 'Gadlys' is also associated with the campaign of 1157. Gadlys (in Bagillt Fechan) is believed to take its name from the Welsh language, *cadlys* meaning a camp or headquarters. An entry in *The Royal Commission on Ancient and Historical Monuments and Constructions, An Inventory of the Ancient Monuments in Wales* (1911) records,

> The two fields on the farm of Gadlys in the township of Bagillt Fechan, called on the Ordnance Map "Bryn Dychwelwch" are supposed to be the place where, after the battle of Coleshill, Owain Gwynedd, in 1157, sounded a retreat.

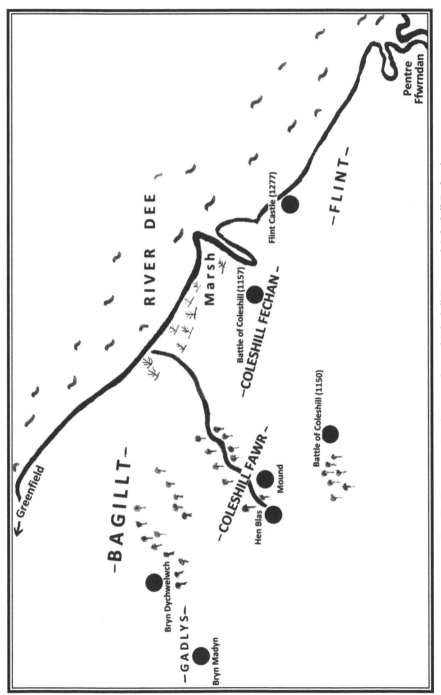

Bagillt (incorporating the townships of Coleshill Fawr and Coleshill Fechan)

According to T. A. Glenn, the battle of 1157 took place in the pass or meadow between Llys Edwin (in present day Northop) and Bryn Edwin (in present day Flint Mountain), a spot now occupied by a stretch of the A55 North Wales Expressway.

Hen Gadlys

Gadlys so full of history,
As its name in Welsh implied.
Where Henry, king of England,
Came to fight and nearly died.
On a hill called Bryn Dychwelwch,
Came the order to retreat.
It was Eleven Fifty Seven,
And an army faced defeat.

In the fury of the battle,
When neither side would yield.
The blood of Celt and Saxon,
Stained red the battle field.
As we walk around the Gadlys
All signs of battle gone.
Remember those who fell here,
Their duty sealed and done.

Norman Watson

These same two fields are also mentioned in *The History of the Parishes of Whitford and Holywell* written by the locally-born writer and antiquarian

Thomas Pennant in 1796, but this time it is Henry II who is ordering his forces to retreat,

> Between this place and Pentre Bagillt, so named from Bryn, a hill, and Dychwelwch, return ! being traditionally said to have been the place from which Henry II gave his order to retreat, when he was engaged with the Welsh, in 1157, with his whole army, in Coleshill, in the same difficulties as he had just before experienced in the depth of Coed Eulo.

Another intriguing local oral tradition relates to a prominent ridge overlooking the two fields of Bryn Dychwelwch. The ridge is currently crowned by the residence of Bryn Madyn Hall, a Georgian country house built in the 1730s for a local wealthy mining entrepreneur. Adjacent to this elegant property is a small wood deliberately enclosed by a perimeter fence. The local tradition declares this wood to be the burial ground of the dead combatants who fell in the vicinity during the campaign of 1157. Many military historians

Bryn Madyn, Bagillt, Flintshire. Overlooking the two fields called Bryn Dychwelwch is a prominent ridge crowned by Bryn Madyn Hall and a small enclosed wood. According to local tradition and the present landholders of the Gadlys estate, the wood is the burial ground of those killed in 1157.

have suggested that the main concentration of burials would be at the point where the main engagement began, and the present landholding family of the Gadlys estate, whose family have farmed and lived at Gadlys for many generations, are insistent that the small secluded wood in their private ownership represents a war cemetery and is the sacred resting place of the soldiers killed in 1157. As owners of this wood, however, the family have always resisted the temptation of proving this tradition via excavation, choosing instead to respect the dignity of those they believe are interred there. Furthermore, the same family are aware of another local tradition that a Welsh force was stationed on the brow of Bryn Madyn hill, the location of the war cemetery, in order to attack Henry II's forces as they swept through the area.

Folklore, tradition and fact are often confused and merged together, and should be treated with extreme caution. Perhaps only as the two Anglo-Norman columns approached his camp at Basingwerk (Coleshill Fawr) did Owain Gwynedd realise the strength of the forces that were ranged against him and, knowing the limitations of his own army, wisely elected to vacate the encampment, a manoeuvre confirmed by the chronicles. The idea of Owain establishing his personal quarters at Gadlys, a position approximately half-a-mile to the west of the established Welsh entrenchments at Basingwerk, is certainly feasible and, as he withdrew from these quarters, it is possible to imagine a Welsh force positioned on Bryn Madyn hill to protect Owain's retreat which would have made sound military sense. Speculating further, any subsequent clash between the opposing forces would probably have caused considerable Welsh casualties in the vicinity of Bryn Madyn — the location of of the supposed burial ground— and Bryn Dychwelwch (local tradition calls it the Hill of Retreat). It is also possible that the Anglo-Norman force that marched against the Welsh camp along the marshy coastal road (an established route later mentioned by Geraldus Cambrensis) engaged a force of Welsh soldiers planted on the Dee coast in the vicinity of Coleshill

Fechan at the location marked on the O.S. map as 'Supposed site of the battle of Coleshill, 1157'. All this is, however, pure speculation and there is no way of telling precisely what occurred when Owain Gwynedd withdrew from his camp. Finally, to muddy the waters even further, there is a possibility that the earlier battle of Coleshill (fought in 1150) has somehow become intertwined with the battle of 1157 as a result of which the mists of many centuries have distorted local tradition and the truth.

When the first bands of Henry's soldiers entered the area of the deserted Welsh camp, the pickings must have been relatively meagre. The ground ploughed up by horses and carts and men probably lay strewn with tattered clothing, rusting mail, partially devoured animal carcasses and capsized wooden casks devoid of their contents. Blackened cooking utensils and small piles of grey ash, some still smouldering, courted company with an abandoned broken cart or two, their loads hurriedly stripped bare by Owain's fleeing soldiers. Geraldus Cambrensis would later describe in telling detail a scene of post-battle during this same campaign.

Bryn Dychwelwch, Bagillt, Flintshire. In the Gadlys area of Bagillt there are two fields known as Bryn Dychwelwch where, according to local tradition, Owain Gwynedd ordered his troops to retreat after the Battle of Coleshill (1157).

In this wood of Coleshulle, a young Welshman was killed while passing through the king's army; the grey-hound who accompanied him did not desert his master's corpse for eight days, though without food; but faithfully defended it from the attacks of dogs, wolves, and birds of prey, with a wonderful attachment. What son to his father, what Nisus to Euryalus, what Polynices to Tydeus, what Orestes to Pylades, would have shown such an affectionate regard? As a mark of favour to the dog, the English, although bitter enemies to the Welsh, ordered the body, now nearly putrid, to be deposited in the ground with the accustomed offices of humanity.

As the said grey-hound faithfully guarded his master's corpse, Owain Gwynedd, a man renowned for his unwavering spirit, led his retreating army to a place of safety and thenceforward continued the campaign against Henry's invading force.

As the two royal armies moved westwards towards the banks of the river

The old Roman road at Oakenholt, Flint. In 2013, in the area of Pentre Ffwrndan (Croes Atti), east of Flint, builders unearthed a well-preserved section of Roman road which ran parallel to the A548 coast road.It is tempting to suggest that this served the Anglo-Norman invaders of 1157.

Clwyd, the course of the war entered a new phase. Although the Welsh ambush upon Henry's column was considered to be a notable success, it served only to delay the inevitable encirclement of Owain Gwynedd's entrenchments at Basingwerk (Coleshill).

Undertaking a methodical march to the castle at Rhuddlan, a strategically important fortress situated on the lowest crossing point of the river Clwyd, Henry's forces had merged into one mighty unit. Although the actual route from Basingwerk to Rhuddlan used by the Anglo-Norman army is not recorded by any of the chronicles, it is plausible that, upon leaving the area of Coleshill, the Anglo-Norman army detached itself from the coast of northern Wales and followed an inland route. Similarly, it may also be considered that the Welsh army mirrored their enemy's inland manoeuvre and deliberately marched in a parallel formation to their foes. The Welsh chronicle, *Brut y Tywysogyon, Red Book of Hergest*, records the progress of both armies at this stage of the campaign:

> [Owain] retreated as far as the place that was called Cil Owen (Kil Ywein). And then the king gathered his host together and went as far as Rhuddlan. And then Owain encamped at Tal-llwyn Pina (Llwynn Pina).

The earliest recorded reference to a place named Cil Owen (or Kil Owain) is 'Chilven' in the Domesday Survey of 1086, where it is recorded as a *berewick* (a subsidiary or outlying estate) of the manor of Rhuddlan. Located one-and-a-half miles to the south-east of the church of St Asaph, the land of Cil Owen lies close to the rivers Clwyd and Elwy, where traditional fording points of both rivers are to be found nearby. Beyond these fords it is believed that an old Roman road led westwards towards Betws-yn-Rhos in the *cantref* (hundred) of Rhos (the district between the rivers Elwy, Clwyd, Conwy and the sea). A local tradition, reported to the author by Mr R. L. Williams, a landowner and businessman whose properties are situated at Cil Owen,

Cil Owen, Waen, St Asaph, Denbighshire. Following the ambush of Henry II, Owain led his troops westwards towards St Asaph. Brut y Tywysogyon notes that he initially retreated to 'Kil Ywein (Cil Owen), on the banks of the river Clwyd and close to the river Elwy, where traditional fording points were located.

maintains that a Welsh prince named Owain hid his army upon the banks of the river Clwyd in the sheltered station of Cil Owen. Even today, Cil Owen's green, rolling meadows present a truly secluded landscape; and it is not too difficult to imagine an army stationed there in order to recuperate prior to resuming a demanding military campaign.

Whatever the route, Henry II eventually swept into the castle at Rhuddlan unopposed. The name Rhuddlan should be translated as 'red bank', and is derived from the red colour of the soil on the river bank. The established stronghold occupying the east bank of the river Clwyd had long been a place of settlement and the strategic site became Henry's new field headquarters. During the eleventh century, the fortification was held at different times by two of the most bloodthirsty characters of the age, namely the Welsh ruler Gruffudd ap Llywelyn (d. 1063), and the Norman lord, Robert of Rhuddlan (d. 1093). Shortly after the Norman Conquest of England, a borough was founded at Rhuddlan comprising a church, a mint and defences that ringed a settlement of seven hectares. To what degree Rhuddlan prospered under Norman (or Anglo-Norman) control is unknown, but in 1140 the garrison fell to Owain Gwynedd. As Henry's ranks settled into life in a new camp, the surrounding marshes and hills were viewed with tremendous suspicion. Likewise, inside the nerve centre of the nearby Welsh camp, Owain Gwynedd must have cut a restless figure. Patently aware that Henry had seized the Rhuddlan citadel without a Welsh spear being raised in anger, Owain's next move could prove decisive. Protecting his outnumbered army from the direct clash of arms which would see it resoundingly shattered, he prudently moved his forces beyond Henry's reach by crossing the Clwyd and Elwy rivers into the neighbouring *cantref*. According to *Brut y Tywysogyn, the Red Book of Hergest*, Owain and his army crossed into the neighbouring *cantref* of Rhos, establishing themselves at a station called Tal-Llwyn Pina (*The Red Book of Hergest*) or Tal-Llwyn Pennant (*Brenhinedd y Saeason*).

Coleshill, supposed site of the battle of 1157, near Flint. The spot marked on the Ordnance Survey map as 'supposed site of Battle of Coleshill (fought in 1157)' was largely built over by the Kimberley Clark company from the 1980s. However, according to a local tradition, any one (or even all) of the adjoining fields in the township of Coleshill Fechan could be the location of the battle.

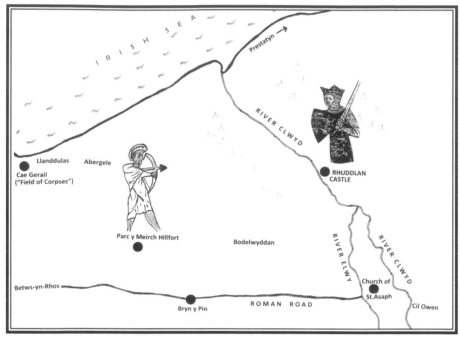

The second phase of the hostilities of 1157.

In response to the occupation of Rhuddlan by Henry's forces, Owain had tactically steered his army to a location where it was to remain until the termination of the campaign. Yet again, the significant question which arises is where was this location known as Tal llwyn Pina or Tal Llwyn Pennant? Traditionally, the site is identified in David Powel's book as 'Bryn y Pin' above Kinmel, which certainly fits in well with the geography of the campaign. It is also worth noting an intriguing statement written by D. R. Thomas in his letter to *Archaeologia Cambrensis* (Fourth Series, XX, October 1874, p 338).

... there are no traces of either a camp or an entrenchment at Bryn-y-Pin; but a very remarkable one at Parc-y-Meirch, which is about two miles distant. Probably the solution of the misstatement is that Owain Gwynedd made his rendezvous at Bryn-y-Pin on his retreat before Henry II, and fixed camp at the strong adjoining point of Parc-y-Meirch. This would be more the likely, as at Bryn-y-Pin he would reach the first elevated and commanding spot after leaving the country subject to Rhuddlan Castle; and he would, moreover, have the old Roman road behind him, if he were not then actually upon it, with a safe retreat further into the interior.

If this bold account is correct, then Owain Gwynedd would have found at Parc-y-Meirch a ready-made, impregnable entrenchment which commanded the only pass by which Henry could reach the Roman road from the low coastal land. D. R. Thomas's account continues —

The house at Bryn-y-Pin is peculiar in having a round tower in its centre, around which the staircase winds, and all the fireplaces are ranged; possibly the very 'Pinna', or its representative, of some old Roman column which served to form the gathering-point on that and many similar occasions.

The historic hillfort known as Parc-y-Meirch, situated near to the village of St George (Llansan Sior), near Abergele, is sometimes referred to as Dinorben Iron Age Hillfort. It has been largely destroyed by quarrying

Bryn-y-Pin, near Glascoed, Denbighshire. Owain led his army from Cil Owen to Tal-llwyn Pina or Tal-llwyn Pennant. The normal identification of this place is Bryn-y-Pin, a station standing on the ancient Roman road some four miles west of St Asaph.

Parc-y-Meirch (Dinorben Hillfort), St George, Abergele. It is highly unlikely that an astute tactician such as Owain Gwynedd would have neglected to use this strong position. Much of the hillfort has now been destroyed by quarrying.

conducted between the 1950s and the late 1970s. Archaeological investigations, however, suggest that the interior of the fort measured some five and a half acres and occupation began during the Mesolithic period in the ninth century BC and continued into the Iron Age, with further activity in the Roman period during the third and fourth centuries AD and into the early mediaeval period. In the absence of any firm evidence, the supposition that Owain Gwynedd established a battle camp on the summit of Parc-y-Meirch should be treated with caution. Nevertheless, a decision to place a camp upon this elevated position (550 feet above sea level) would have made perfect military sense. The site was well protected on all sides except the south, and and was located only four miles from Rhuddlan. It would have formed an excellent observation post for monitoring the movements of an enemy encamped at Rhuddlan. Furthermore, it is highly unlikely that an experienced military tactician such as Owain Gwynedd would have chosen to neglect such a strategically blessed site. Interestingly, the area surrounding the ancient hillfort contains many relics of the past, including a Roman road, prehistoric burial mounds and the mediaeval manor of Dinorben Fawr, on the site of the present Dinorben Hall Farm. During the time of the Welsh princes, Dinorben was the main court for the commote of Is Dulas in the *cantref* of Rhos. *An Inventory of the Ancient Monuments in Wales and Monmouthshire – IV, County of Denbigh* (RCAHM&CWM, 1914) duly acknowledges the site's importance:

> A mount might be expected at such a site (Dinorben Hall), but no mound exists. The original Dinorben was undoubtedly the fort on the summit of the hill above Parc-y-Meirch wood.

In the adjoining districts, there are further traditions associated with the campaign of 1157. In the town of Abergele, a local tradition maintains that Owain Gwynedd used a watch tower here to aid his campaign of 1157. The nearby Gwrych Castle estate, built during the early part of the nineteenth century, boasts a number of encircling gate lodges, and at one of these lodges, Tan-yr-Ogo in Llanddulas, there are four sandstone tablets embedded on the arched entrance commemorating historical events that were supposed to have happened at or near to this place. Interestingly, one of them reads,

> In the reign of Henry II, Owen Gwynedd, Prince of North Wales, on retreat from Flintshire, fortified himself in this pass, where he gave battle to the forces of that Monarch and repulsed them with great

Owain Gwynedd as portrayed in a 1909 painting by Hugh Williams (extracted from a commemorative panel at Crogen, Chirk).

slaughter. After having secured this important post, he retreated to Pen y Parc, in the adjoining parish, where he made a stand against the English forces and effectually checked the further invasion of his dominions.

In this same area, a field near to Tan-yr-Ogo Lodge (between Abergele and Llanddulas) is known as Cae Gerail which translates as 'field of the corpses'. A local tradition reveals the area to be the historic scene of many fierce battles between the Welsh and their Saxon and Norman invaders, and according to Mark Baker in *The Rise and Fall of Gwrych Castle, Abergele* (2003), the Tan-yr-Ogo Pass is sometimes named 'the Themopylae of Wales' (Thermopylae being the scene of a notable battle fought in 480 BC between the forces of Greece and Persia). We may never be sure about the origins of such traditions, but they certainly keep alive the area's associations with the campaign of 1157.

The two armies settled into the environment of their new camps: the Anglo-Normans at Rhuddlan, the Welsh at Tal-llwyn Pina. During the days

Tan-yr-Ogo Lodge, Llanddulas, Conwy. Embedded in the wall on either side of the entrance gate are four tablets that bear witness to the reputed bloody history of this locality.

that followed, dogged bands attached to Henry's army manfully attempted to cross the silvery stretch of the Clwyd River. To resist these manoeuvres, equally determined bands of Welsh fighters robustly countered any progress gained by the invaders. Time and again, by daylight and in darkness, Henry's ranks came under attack, fighting for their lives against the merciless arrows, missiles, swords and spears of the Welsh. Henry's troops would have responded in kind, and during a desperate fight for survival in the marshes around Rhuddlan, they maimed, butchered, and repelled their Welsh foes. During this crucial phase of the campaign, the battlefield tactics employed by Owain Gwynedd should be viewed as highly commendable. Any other leader confronted by such overwhelming odds, would be forgiven for organising an outright retreat towards the sanctuary of the Gwynedd heartlands. By ignoring this safer option, Owain chose to make a valiant stand in the killing zone surrounding Rhuddlan in an attempt to prevent the crossing of the Clwyd by Henry's army.

Madog ap Maredudd (d. 1160), the ruler of the Welsh kingdom of Powys, was married to Susanna, the daughter of Gruffudd ap Cynan, and was therefore the brother-in-law of Owain Gwynedd. Under his talented leadership, the kingdom of Powys probably reached its greatest extent and, at the peak of his power, Madog took control of lands as far away as the Fyrnwy and an area which stretched from Arwystli in central Wales to near Chester. He also expanded his kingdom eastwards, seizing Oswestry in 1149, and established his overlordship over Hywel ab Ieuaf, the ruler of Arwystli by 1151. He soon came to realise that in order to rule Powys successfully he had to navigate a middle course between the power of Owain Gwynedd in north Wales and the power of the Anglo-Norman lords in the Marches. Moreover, despite his impressive territorial gains, he had suffered greatly at the hands of his brother-in-law, losing the Powysian commote of Iâl in 1149 to Gwynedd, followed by a resounding defeat at the Battle of Coleshill in 1150. The role played by Madog ap Maredudd during the campaign of 1157 remains the subject of debate. The Welsh chronicle, *Brut y Tywysogyon, Red Book of Hergest*, informs us that '... Madog ap Maredudd, lord of Powys, chose a place for himself to encamp between the king's host and Owain's host, so that he might receive the first assaults the king would make', a statement which clearly indicates an alliance between Powys and Gwynedd. In contrast, *Brenhinedd y Saeson* records that ' Madog, prince of Powys, and a part of the king's host with him, went in ships to Abermenai, and there they invaded Anglesey and pillaged the church of Mary and the church of Peter,' a statement which suggests a union between Powys and England. Modern historians, including R. Geraint Gruffydd, Roger Turvey, Huw Pryce and David Moore, have portrayed Madog as Henry's ally. In *The Acts of Welsh Rulers 1120–1283*, Huw Pryce (2005), states that '... Madog and Hywel (ab Ieuaf), together with Madog's brother Iorwerth Goch, joined Henry II in his campaign against Owain Gwynedd.' Roger Turvey in *Twenty-one Welsh Princes* (2010), shares this view — 'In 1157 Madog, together with his client Hywel ab Ieuaf of Arwystli, joined in Henry II's successful campaign against Owain Gwynedd. Madog's reward was both political and financial, for in supporting the king he acquired a guarantor of his kingdom's security along with substantial payments from the English exchequer.' In relation to these payments, David Moore, author of *The Welsh Wars of Independence* (2007), writes — 'Thus Madog received £8 in Henry II's service in 1157, and Iorwerth (Goch) was given 40 shillings and the manor of Sutton in Shropshire for his part in the campaign, while the king enabled Madog's sons to procure arms for the war, and Owain Cyfeiliog may have received 5 marks from Henry in 1157 and 15 shillings in 1160.' Similarly, the article 'A Welsh Poet falls at the battle of Coleshill, 1157' written by R. Geraint Gruffydd (*Flintshire Historical Society Journal*, v 36, 2003), also places Madog firmly in the corner of Henry II.

Factors in his [Henry II's] favour included the defection of Owain Gwynedd's brother Cadwaladr, who had lived as an exile in England since 1152; the fact that the Earl of Chester was a minor in royal wardship; and the (not unexpected) adherence of Powys to the Anglo-Norman cause, symbolised by payments made to its king, Madog ap Maredudd, his borther Iorwerth Goch, and the sub-king of Arwystli, Hywel ab Ieuaf, which are duly recorded in the Pipe Rolls.

This account is centred on an elegy written by Cynddelw Brydydd Mawr honouring a Powysian warrior killed in the fighting of 1157 and includes the following passage — 'It should be stressed that [our] Bleddyn Fardd (the deceased) was a member of the Powys contingent which was fighting under the leadership of Madog ap Maredudd as part of Henry's army against Gwynedd.'

As the ongoing hostilities revolved around Rhuddlan, additional battle lines were soon to be drawn elsewhere, resulting in further bloodshed.

12

Slicing through the grey-green waters of the Irish Sea, an Anglo-Norman fleet made steady progress towards the island of Anglesey. The soldiers that crowded the decks would soon be treated to the sight of the beautiful island. The historic isle is the most northerly part of Wales and is home to long expanses of sand, majestic cliffs, sheltered coves and, bursting out from almost every crevice along its coast are flowers of every colour. During the mediaeval period, Anglesey was renowned as the most important growing area in Wales and, it was noted by Geraldus Cambrensis that 'When crops have failed in all other regions, this island, from the richness of its soil and its abundant produce, has been able to supply all of Wales'. Even today, the

St Beuno's Church, Aberffraw, Anglesey. A section of masonry within this church is all that remains of the royal court.

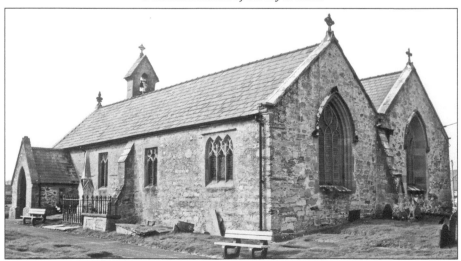

Mediaeval ships as shown in the eleventh-century Bayeux Tapestry.

island's motto '*Môn, Mam Cymru*' is an epithet meaning 'Anglesey, Mother of Wales'. During the lifetime of the royal house of Gwynedd, the island formed the kingdom's spiritual and economic heart and the royal court of Aberffraw, on the south-west coast, formed the principal seat of the dynasty's rulers. Serving the ruler's daily needs, were a hall, a chapel, stables, barns, byres and a mill. The river Ffraw meets the sea here where an endless supply of fresh fish provided daily nourishment for the king's household. In the fields surrounding the *llys* (court) at Aberffraw, grazing sheep and herds of cattle and home-bred ponies greeted the eyes of those visiting the royal court. Here the royal chapel was built in stone in the Romanesque manner, the carved arch that divided the nave from the chancel boasting an elaborate design of chevrons and animal heads. The native rulers of mediaeval Wales took their religion seriously and were as active in founding and constructing religious houses as they were in building fortified manors and castles, a policy undoubtedly fuelled by the hope and belief of securing for themselves an eternal place in the afterlife. The priory church at Penmon, the tower at Llaneilian and a portion of the parish church of Aberffraw all relate to the period of Owain's reign.

Aboard the ships, battle-hardened soldiers, their heads crowned by domes of iron, stood shoulder to shoulder with the mail-coated sons of wealthy lords primed to wage war. During the reign of Henry II, fleets played a vital role in warfare. The overall size of the Anglo-Norman marine force of 1157 remains a subject of speculation. An Anglo-Norman expedition of May 1170, led by Raymond le Gros, landed at Baginbun Head in Wexford, Ireland, and was said to have included 300 foot archers, 100 mounted archers and 30 knights. During the autumn of 1171, Henry himself led an expeditionary force to Ireland which disembarked at Waterford and consisted of 4,000 men-at-arms and archers and 500 mounted knights. The command of such fleets went, as a general rule, not to men with lengthy experience of the sea, but to soldiers. It is impossible to be certain, but the appearance of Henry FitzHenry, an illegitimate son of King Henry I of England (the uncle of Henry II), in the midst of the marine force of 1157 would seem to indicate that the supreme command was his. According to contemporary Welsh poetry, the Anglo-Norman fleet that sailed menacingly towards Anglesey totalled three navies. The words of the warrior poet Gwalchmai ap Meilyr (d. 1170) are worth noting:

> Three legions came, sea-surge's vessels,
>
> Three strong navies seeking to crush him.
>
> One from Ireland, a second with soldiers
>
> From the Norsemen, long prows of the deep,
>
> And the third sailing from Normandy....

On this basis, one might conclude that the almost limitless resources of the Crown conspired to create an impressive fleet of ships providing crucial off-shore support to Henry's land army as it advanced along the coast of northern Wales.

As the bows of the leading ships approached the coast, the travelling contingent must have viewed the outstretched coastline with natural suspicion. But, those on board the ships would have been buoyed by the

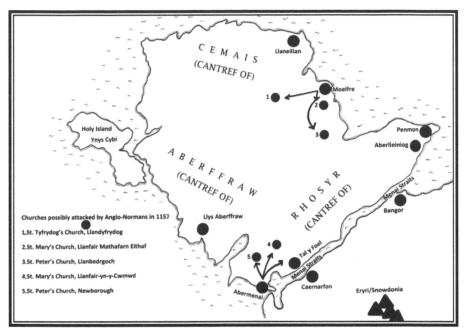

Anglesey (Ynys Môn), 1157

knowledge that Owain Gwynedd's army occupied a distant station some forty or more miles away in the area of Rhuddlan, and the chances of an armed Welsh response to the invading naval force were considered extremely remote. As the fleet dropped anchor, disembarkation began and a riotous mixture of men and horses plunged theatrically into the ice cold shallows. The men waded to the shore clutching their weapons and bundles of kit, and rolls of luggage were tossed freely overboard to drift towards the shore.

Setting foot on dry land, Henry's marine force did not encounter so much as a hostile spear, arrow, or missile hurled in their direction, a signal clearly viewed by the invaders as a licence to begin a campaign of terror. In the ninth century, Vikings from Scandinavia had raided parts of Anglesey, and during these terrifying incursions, churches had been plundered, cattle and ships stolen and scores of native inhabitants carried into captivity as slaves. In 1157, the reported ill-deeds of the Anglo-Normans on Anglesey mirrored

*Llanbedrgoch
Church*

*Llanfairmathafarn
Eithaf Church*

*Llandyfrydog
Church*

those atrocities committed by their fearsome ancestors and mayhem reigned supreme as religious houses in the vicinity were plundered of their contents and other sacred items were either damaged or destroyed. As the shocking scenes of desecration ended, the satisfied soldiers moved away, leaving behind a landscape of smoking ruins. As the day ended, the marauders on Môn settled down for the night. However, unbeknown to them, a force of Welshmen was gathering intent on delivering vengeance the following day.

According to *Brut y Tywysogyon, Red Book of Hergest*, the king's fleet had 'pillaged the church of Mary and the church of Peter and many other churches.' The two named churches are popularly assumed to represent the churches of Llanbedr-goch (Peter) and Llanfair Mathafarn Eithaf (Mary). According to Geraldus Cambrensis, the church of St Tyfrydog in Llandyfrydog was also despoiled, and all three churches are located in the same district, not far from the island's eastern coast.

The day after the landing, a force of Welshmen native to the island savagely attacked the unsuspecting Anglo-Normans. Fuelled by vengeance, they set about their startled enemy and the butchery that followed proved disastrous for the invaders. When describing this battle, the Welsh chronicles leave us in no doubt as to whom the victory belonged.

For on the following day a battle took place between them and the men of Anglesey; and in that battle the French fled, according to their usual custom, after many of them had been slain and others had been captured and others had been drowned. And it was with difficulty that a few of them escaped to the ships after Henry, son of King Henry [the first] and most of the chief officers of the ships had been slain. [*Brut y Tywysogyon. Red Book of Hergest*]

The Anglo-Norman invasion of Anglesey should perhaps be measured in corpses rather than miles. Many of their number were killed on the shoreline while others were despatched to a watery grave. According to Geraldus Cambrensis, the level of violence directed against the raiders was God's punishment for the desecration of holy sites on the island. This sensational Welsh victory on Anglesey became known to history as the Battle of Tal-y-Moelfre, an encounter commonly identified with the village and small harbour of Moelfre on Anglesey's north-eastern coast. When penning a spirited ode in celebration of the great victory, the Welsh royal court poet Gwalchmai ap Meilyr appears to fix the battle to Tal-y-Moelfre, 'And a thousand war-shouts about Tal-y-Moelfre.'

The Battle of Tal-y-Moelfre

The generous chief I sing of Rhodri's line,
With princely gifts endow'd, whose hand
Hath often curb'd the border land,
Owain, great heir of Britain's throne;
Whom fair ambition marks her own,
Who ne'er to yield to man was known;
Nor heaps he stores at Avarice's shrine.

Three mighty legions o'er the sea-flood came,
Three fleets intent on sudden fray;
One from Erin's verdant coast,
One with Lochlin's armed host,
Long burdens of the billowy way;
The third, from far, bore them of Norman name,
To fruitless labour doom'd, and barren fame.

Gainst Mona's gallant lord, where lo! he stands,
His warlike sons ranged at his side,
Rushes the dark tumultuous tide,
Th' insulting tempest of the hostile bands:
Boldly he turns the furious storm,
Before him wild confusion flies,
While havoc rears her hideous form,
And prostrate rank expiring lies;
Conflict upon conflict growing,
Gore upon gore in torrents flowing,
Shrieks answering shrieks, and slaughter raving,
And high o'er Moelfre's front a thousand banners waving.
Now thickens still the frantic war,
The flashing death-strokes gleam afar,
Spear rings on spear, flight urges flight,

And drowning victims plunge to night;
Check'd by the torrent – tide of blood,
Backward Menai rolls his flood;
The mailed wariors on the shore,
With carnage strew'd, and dyed with gore,
In awful anguish drag their mangled limbs along,
And high the slaughter'd throng
Is heap'd, the King's red chiefs before.

Lloegria's onset thus, Lloegria's flight,
The struggle doom'd her power to tame,
Shall, with her routed sons, unite
To raise great Owain's sword to fame;
Whilst sevenscore tongues of his exploits shall tell,
And all their high renown through future ages swell.

Gwallchmai ap Meilyr (d c.1180)

There exists, however, a degree of uncertainty as to exactly where the battle took place. The text of *Brenhinedd y Saeson* identifies Aber Menai as the landing place of the Anglo-Norman fleet, an important harbour during the age of the Welsh princes, guarding the western entrance to the Menai Strait. Interestingly, in the hinterland near Tal-y-Foel on the Menai Strait there exist mediaeval churches dedicated to Mary and Peter — Saint Mary's Church at Llanfair-yn-y-Cwmwd and Saint Peter's Church at Newborough. Both Gwalchmai ap Meilyr and Hywel ab Owain Gwynedd in their poems celebrated the victory and made reference to the Menai Strait — 'And Menai ebbed not, for the inflowing of the streams of blood' (Gwalchmai ap Meilyr), 'and a beardless warrior put to flight a thousand leaders on Menai Water' (Hywel ab Owain Gwynedd).

Another mystery concerning the battle on Anglesey is the identity of the Welsh force that inflicted such savagery upon the raiders. The Welsh chronicles refer to those responsible for the reported slaughter of so many of the invading soldiers as 'the youth of Anglesey' and 'the men of Anglesey', but who in fact were these defenders of the island and under whose command did they operate so successfully?

A number of historians have theorised that Owain, on leaving his Aberffraw court to pursue the scent of war, must have taken the cream, if not all, of his military strength with him in order to face the king of England on the mainland in north-east Wales. The idea that Owain Gwynedd might have deliberately maintained an armed force on Anglesey to protect his kingdom's capital is, however, certainly plausible. Furthermore, during the campaign of 1157, Hywel ab Owain Gwynedd, another of Owain Gwynedd's sons, was regarded as a fearless and vastly experienced warrior who is widely regarded by historians as his father's intended successor. With the military resources of Gwynedd stretched, a number of writers speculate that it was Hywel who played a prominent role in the successful defence of Anglesey. Writing in *The Poets of the Welsh Princes* (Writers of Wales series, 1994), J. E. Caerwyn Williams suggests that 'Owain Gwynedd's son, Hywel ab Owain Gwynedd, must have taken part in the battle of Tal-y-Moelfre for we have a poem by him —he is in all probability the "beardless champion at Menai"', and Sean Davies, in *War and Society in Mediaeval Wales, 622-1283, Welsh Military Institutions* (2014) states that 'It seems that another son, Hywel, had been left to organise the defence of Anglesey.'

13

Inside the confines of his Rhuddlan headquarters, King Henry received the shocking news of his troops' calamitous defeat on Anglesey. From that pivotal moment onwards, the hostilities drew to a close, paving the way for the high drama of a decisive truce summit at Rhuddlan. It is unknown which royal commander instigated the truce, but the flavour of the subsequent political settlement certainly favoured King Henry. No details have survived as to whether or not the two rival commanders ever came face to face at the Rhuddlan summit, but we can certainly envisage a mounted delegation of Welsh soldiers leaving Owain's camp to confer with Henry or his elected representatives. Regardless of which side called for the truce, the agreed cessation of hostilities certainly suited both sides equally. Despite recording a sensational victory against Henry and his household troop at the start of the campaign in the woods of Tegeingl, the army of Gwynedd had subsequently been forced to retreat as far westwards as the river Clwyd, thereby relinquishing Owain's recent territorial gains in Tegeingl. Moreover, despite the recording of a second triumph over the invaders at the battle on Anglesey, any continuation of the Welsh war effort would suffer greatly from the effects of being hopelessly outstretched and heavily outnumbered; the boldness and sheer bravery of the Welsh resistance thus far failing to even dent Henry's great numerical advantages in both men and resources. Likewise, from the Anglo-Norman point of view, Henry's well-planned campaign had not proved entirely fruitful; suffering a ferocious assault early in the campaign at a location only a short distance away from the royal camp at Chester, the king

Twt Hill (Old Rhuddlan Castle), Rhuddlan, Denbighshire. Occupying a natural spur above the river Clwyd, this eleventh-century earthwork motte and bailey castle was captured by Owain Gwynedd c.1150. Retaken in 1157 by Henry II, the king was to receive no respite here as Welsh fighters harassed the invading army 'both by day and by night.' It was while at Rhuddlan that Henry received the news of his army's defeat on Anglesey, paving the way for a peace summit at the castle.

had personally witnessed the destructive force of Welsh aggression, and in the wake of the ambush in which Henry narrowly escaped with his life, had found himself marooned at the fortress in Rhuddlan, the location of his camp becoming a daily target for resolute bands of Welsh fighters. Unwilling, or simply unable, to cross the river Clwyd into the interior of Owain Gwynedd's kingdom, Henry had failed to register a single victory over Owain's forces on either land or sea.

One source reveals the peace was settled around the time of the feast of John the Baptist, 29th August, an indication that the campaign had lasted for a period of about six weeks, a span of time equating to the length of military service usually owed to a feudal overlord.

As the wheels of Henry's war machine shuddered to a halt, so the journey homewards began for the warriors of Gwynedd. The bloodied, maimed and wearied veterans of the campaign trudged westwards towards the heartland of Gwynedd, situated beyond the Conwy River. Their commander, Owain Gwynedd, had evidently agreed to the numerous Anglo-Norman demands. In an attempt to weaken the power of Gwynedd and the prestige of its ruler, King Henry and his ermine-robed ministers had chosen their terms wisely. By submitting to Henry's will, Owain Gwynedd gave homage to the King of England (the precise manner of the *hominium* is not recorded). He was also forced to deliver into Henry's custody two of his young sons as hostages, a traditional measure designed purely to secure the future good conduct of a dangerous adversary (the two sons are commonly identified as Cadwallon and Cynwrig). In addition, Owain was ordered to restore Cadwaladr, his exiled younger brother and recent opponent, to his former territories. During a chequered career, Cadwaladr had held territories in Anglesey, northern Ceredigion, Meirionnydd, Llŷn, and Ness in Shropshire, but not simultaneously. Owain was also forced to surrender his recent territorial gains in Tegeingl, a *cantref* traditionally claimed by the kingdom of Gwynedd.

Throughout Wales, the fall-out from the war's political settlement had a profound effect. The castles of Rhuddlan, Prestatyn and Basingwerk in Tegeingl became Anglo-Norman castles and were either rebuilt or refortified in order to maintain the Crown's vice-like grip on the north-east corner of Wales. Shortly after the termination of the hostilities, Owain's woes were intensified when he incurred additional territorial losses; the castle that he had erected in 1149 in the seized commote of Iâl was attacked by Iorwerth Goch, brother of Madog ap Maredudd of Powys, and by taking full advantage of the constraints laid upon the ruler of Gwynedd, returned the *commote* to Powysian hands.

For the next eight years, Owain Gwynedd adopted the role of a fully compliant vassal to Henry's Crown. In 1159, an Anglo-Norman army led by Reginald, earl of Cornwall, the illegitimate son of Henry I and uncle to Henry II, invaded south-west Wales so as to subdue the rising threat of the Lord

Rhys, the ruler of the Welsh kingdom of Deheubarth. As part of his obligation to Henry, Owain dutifully sent forces from Gwynedd under the command of his sons, Hywel and Cynan, to assist in the campaign against his ambitious nephew, the Lord Rhys. One year later, Owain delivered the captured Welsh lord, Einion Clud (d. 1177) of Maelienydd, a *cantref* in central Wales, to Crown officials who subsequently detained the Welshman inside the secure walls of Worcester Castle. During the early part of 1163, Henry II invaded south-west Wales himself in order to once again subdue the irrepressible Lord Rhys. Surprisingly, the campaign did not erupt into full-scale hostilities and, following Owain's advice, the Lord Rhys surrendered to Henry and accompanied the king to England.

In a further demonstration of his binding allegiance to the terms of the treaty of 1157, Owain dutifully attended the king's council session at Woodstock on 1st July, 1163. He was not alone. In the words of Ralph of Diceto, a dean of St Paul's Cathedral and the author of two mediaeval chronicles, the royal session was attended by 'Malcolm king of the Scots, Rhys prince of the southern Welsh, Owain of the northern, and five of the greater men of Wales' each of them rendering homage to the king of England and to Henry his son.

At this stage of Owain Gwynedd's colourful career, an ageing prince's reluctance to take up arms could easily be understood; a wish for peace as he inched his way closer towards the end of his life was surely a welcome prospect. Owain , however, despite being shackled to the terms of Henry's suzerainty, continued to flex his considerable muscle as Wales' dominant prince. After the death of Madog ap Maredudd of Powys in 1160, Owain occupied the commote of Edeirnion (in the Powysian *cantref* of Penllyn) and two years later launched an attack against Hywel ab Ieuaf, ruler of Arwystli (a *cantref* in central Wales), recording a victory at Llandinam. Evidently, Owain's ripening years had failed to diminish a steely determination to secure supremacy over his fellow Welsh rulers.

Early in 1165, his son, Dafydd, crossed the river Clwyd to invade the cantref of Tegeingl, threatening the royal castles there, before returning to Gwynedd with plunder and captives. This sudden blow from the direction of Gwynedd infuriated Henry and shattered any illusions of peaceful relations between the English Crown and the northern Welsh. During this same eventful period, Owain adopted the new title of Prince. In two of three surviving letters written in the 1160s to Louis VII, king of France, Owain styles himself as *rex Walie* (king of Wales). In the third letter, he asserts himself as Waliarum princeps (prince of Wales). The use of this elevated title is believed to be the first by any Welsh ruler.

Owain's expanding confidence gave rise to an attempt to form a Franco-Welsh alliance against Henry II and he thereby became the first Welsh ruler known to seek an alliance with the ruler of a continental power. Inevitably, Owain's calculated revival provoked the activation of another major royal campaign in northern Wales. The stage was set for a final clash of arms between Owain and Henry.

14

During the summer of 1165, King Henry II gathered a mighty force of soldiers at Oswestry for the purpose of invading northern Wales, the native chronicles describing its strength as 'a host beyond number of the picked warriors of England and Normandy and Flanders and Gascony and Anjou and all the North and Scotland.' It was arguably the largest invasion force ever mustered by a ruling king of England. Once again, his intricate planning for such an important national campaign was meticulous. For example, on corn alone, payments were made in Gloucestershire for 849 horse-loads, in Lincolnshire for 235.5 sesters [1 sester equalled about 12 bushels], in Oxfordshire and Berkshire for 1,000 horse-loads, and in Worcestershire for 509 horse-loads, to be carried to Shrewsbury.

In response to this gargantuan threat, the native rulers of Wales, in a rare display of unity, welded together their respective forces to form an impressive national coalition of warriors. With the talismanic Owain Gwynedd as its commander, the Welsh army initially gathered at Corwen in the valley of the Dee and its ranks included Owain and Cadwaladr with the troops of Gwynedd; the Lord Rhys from Deheubarth in south-west Wales; Owain Cyfeiliog, Iorwerth Goch and all the sons of Madog ap Maredudd with the entire force of Powys; and the sons of Madog ab Idnerth, Cadwallon ap Madog and the liberated Einion Clud, with the warriors of Maelienydd and Elfael in central Wales. Only the princes of Gwent and Glamorgan in south-east Wales resisted the allure of this unprecedented national alliance.

When Henry's army crossed into Wales along the river Ceiriog in north-

Battle of Crogen, 1165. This commemorative plaque is on Castle Mill Bridge, near Chirk, Wrexham. In the summer of 1165, Henry II again invaded Wales, 'to annihilate all Welshmen'. He was attacked at Crogen and defeated by a coalition of Welsh forces.

east Wales, the size of the Welsh army's task must have been daunting. Despite the strength of the Anglo-Norman forces, the campaign proved completely disastrous for Henry, and probing bands of Welsh fighters mercilessly harried his heavily-laden army as it made its way through the narrow Ceiriog valley. To heap more misery on Henry's fortunes, an unseasonably wet Welsh summer caused the invaders further hindrance and torment, dashing all hopes of sweeping success.

Faced with little alternative, Henry ordered a mass retreat to escape the uncompromising landscape of rain lashed mountains, sodden bogs and dense forests. Understandably enraged by his failure to crush the unified forces of Wales, he reacted by ordering that the twenty-two Welsh royal hostages he had held in England, and who had accompanied the royal army on the campaign trail, should be mutilated. Among those horribly blinded and possibly castrated, were Cynwrig and Cadwallon, two of Owain Gwynedd's young sons. Henry also ordered that the noses and ears of the female hostages be slit. This recorded atrocity was an admission of failure, and the thirty-two year old Henry never set foot in Wales again, preferring instead a policy of containment over invasion.

Prestatyn Castle, Denbighshire. Following the cessation of hostilities, the Tegeingl castles of Rhuddlan, Prestatyn and Basingwerk became royal interests and were either rebuilt or refortified. Prestatyn had its own market, mill, granary and nearby harbour, and must have flourished under the stewardship of Robert de Banastre. It was destroyed by Owain Gwynedd in 1167.

After Henry's disastrous Welsh campaign of 1165, Owain Gwynedd was at the height of his power; his dominance was reflected in his letters, rebranding himself as 'prince of the Welsh' and 'prince of Wales'. Sometime during 1166/67, the rejuvenated Owain launched a military campaign in north-east Wales and, taking full advantage of Henry's escalating troubles on the continent, took control of the castles at Basingwerk, Rhuddlan and Prestatyn. In truth, Henry was forced to ignore these latest territorial gains by the ruler of Gwynedd as he was deeply committed to fighting a series of wars and rebellions involving the French, Flemish, Bretons, Gascons, Poitevins and Scots. The extensive pressure exerted on his 'empire' by his enemies forced Henry to cross the Channel to France in the second half of March, 1166, and he remained abroad for four years.

Seeking to forge an alliance with the French king Louis VII (1137–80) against Henry II, Owain Gwynedd despatched at least four diplomatic missions to the French royal court between the autumn of 1164 and the spring of 1166. The confident authority enjoyed by Owain during his final years as ruler of Gwynedd was reflected in his unwavering defiance of obtrusive attempts made by Archbishop Thomas à Becket to secure the election of a bishop of Bangor acceptable to Canterbury. The strong-minded Becket responded by enlisting the support of Pope Alexander II and they vehemently attacked Owain's twenty or so years marriage to Cristin, the daughter of Gronw ab Owain. Cristin was Owain's second wife, but, because she was his first cousin, their matrimonial union was not permitted under canon law and the ruler of Gwynedd was ordered to separate. As the row rumbled on, attempts to resolve the issue through the mediation of Louis VII of France came to nothing. There was hardly a Welsh prince who had not committed the same offence, but owing to Owain's steadfast refusal to buckle and abandon his wife, Becket eventually pronounced the sentence of excommunication upon the ruler of Gwynedd. This damning sentence mattered little to Owain, whose own clergy totally disregarded it, citing above all else that Owain's personal will within his own dominions was law.

On 23rd November, during the year 1170, Owain Gwynedd, the self-proclaimed prince of the Welsh, died. The aged warrior succumbed to natural causes. During a remarkable thirty-three year reign, he was regarded as a fearless warrior, a skilled statesman and a sagacious diplomat. He also secured his dynasty as the leading kingdom in Wales. The eloquent elegies of Daniel ap Llosgwrn, Seisyll Bryffwrch and Cynddelw Brydydd Mawr speak of a man worthy of both admiration and adoration beyond the ordinary. Not surprisingly, he soon acquired the rare epithet *Fawr* (Great). He was devoutly religious and was regarded by his contemporaries as an exceptionally generous patron of the church in Wales. Of course, those clerics whom he patronised repaid his personal faith in them by supporting him in the face of intense pressure applied by king, pope and archbishop. In a written correspondence addressed to Owain, Archbishop Becket acknowledged some of Owain's personal qualities, 'We know that you are a wise man, who knows

A stone tablet (left) in the floor of the south aisle of Bangor Cathedral, informs visitors of Owain's burial within the building.

Bangor Cathedral, Gwynedd. Somewhere inside this ancient building lies the body of Prince Owain Gwynedd.

how to weigh good and evil, right and wrong, with the subtle measure of reason'. Likewise, the words of Geraldus Cambrensis confirm him as a man in possession of extraordinary wisdom:

The leaders of the English army [in the summer of 1165] had burnt down certain Welsh churches, with their villages and churchyards. As a result the sons of Owain Gwynedd, supported by a band of young soldiers who were with them, bitterly harangued their father, and fellow princes, too, swearing that they would never in future spare any English churches. Everyone present was on the point of agreeing to this, but Owain, who was well known among his peers for his great wisdom and moderation, quelled the tumult. 'I do not agree with you at all,' he said. 'On the contrary, we ought to be pleased with what has happened and rejoice. Unless we have God on our side, we are no match for the English. By what they have done they have alienated Him. He can avenge Himself and us, too, in the most striking way. Let us accordingly promise God devoutly that from this moment on we will pay greater reverence and honour than ever before to all churches and holy places'.

Brut y Tywysogyon praises Owain as '... a man of great renown and of infinite prudence and nobility, the bulwark and strength of Wales, unconquered from his youth, after victories beyond number, without having ever refused a man the request that was made to him.' Perhaps, the greatest tribute given to him came at the time of his death, when the sentence of excommunication was totally ignored by his serving clergy when laying the great man to rest inside the hallowed precincts of Bangor Cathedral, the prince's decorated tomb taking pride of place in the wall of the presbytery close to the Great Altar.

Withstanding the external pressures of Marcher ambition and fierce royal intervention, the figure of Owain Gwynedd shall forever be remembered as one of the boldest champions of the national cause in Wales. Furthermore, modern historians justly acclaim him as one of the founding fathers of the Welsh nation, a man who kindled the flame of nationhood against tremendous odds and consistent struggle.

King Henry II lived nineteen years after the death of his old adversary, dying during the thirty-fifth year of his reign on 6th July, 1189, at Chinon Castle in the heart of the Loire Valley in Anjou, France. The closing years of Henry's reign were blighted by personal tragedy and violent conflict. Two of his sons died before their thirtieth birthdays, Henry, known as the 'Young King', died aged 28, in the summer of 1183, during the course of a campaign in the Limousin against his father, and Geoffrey died in Paris during August, 1186, evidence suggesting that the 27-year-old was actively planning another rebellion against his father. After these deaths, a series of armed disputes continued between Henry and his remaining troublesome sons, including both Richard and John, who actively took sides against their father during the bitter feuding. Henry's wife, Eleanor of Aquitaine, spent fifteen years (1174–89) under close arrest, after openly supporting the rebellions of her sons, and another of Henry's personal disputes ended ingloriously, his personal tussle with his close friend Archbishop Thomas à Becket leading to the archbishop's notorious death at the hands of four of Henry's loyal knights (William de Tracey, Reginald Fitzurse, Hugh de Morville and Richard Brito) inside Canterbury Cathedral on the cold evening of 29th December, 1170. Becket's brutal death sent a tremor of horror and outrage throughout mediaeval Europe, and although his murder could not be directly attributed to the king's personal will, Henry was racked with guilt. Four years later, in an act of penance imposed by the Pope, the king donned a sack-cloth and walked barefoot through the streets of Canterbury while eighty monks flogged him with branches. Henry capped his atonement by spending the night in the martyr's crypt. Of his sons, only his illegitimate son, Geoffrey Plantagenet remained by him to the end. Legend maintains that as the 56-year-old Henry lay dying, he called out to Geoffrey, 'You are my true son' and 'the others, they are the bastards'. The day after his death, when he was prepared for a dignified burial, he lay in state wearing a gold crown on his head, gauntlets on his hands, spurs on his feet and a magnificent sword belted to his side. According to *Gesta Henrici Secundi* (The Chronicle of the Reign of Henry II), as his eldest surviving legitimate son, Richard, rushed forth to meet the funeral cortege, a stream of blood suddenly flowed from the dead king's nostrils 'as if his spirit was moved with indignation'. Notwithstanding the manner of Henry's inglorious exit from this earth, his realm of England stood as the true and lasting memorial of his genius.

The tombs of King Henry II and Queen Eleanor in Fontevraud Abbey, Anjou, France.

#0021 - 220518 - C0 - 210/148/10 - PB - 9781844941162